Tyndale House Publishers, Inc.
Wheaton, Illinois

before i dream

bedtime Bible Storybook

Karyn Henley

Edited by Betty Free Swanberg

Designed by Beth Sparkman

Previously published as *Before I Dream Bible Storybook.*

Library of Congress Cataloging-in-Publication Date

Henley, Karen.
  Before I dream bedtime Bible storybook / Karen Henley.
    p. cm.
  Rev. ed. of: Before I dream Bible storybook. c2001.
  ISBN 0-4143-0092-1
  1. Bible stories, English. I. Henley, Karyn. Before I dream Bible storybook. II. Title.
  BS551.3H46 2005
  220.9'505—dc22   2004016271

Printed in Singapore

10 09 08 07 06 05 04
6   5   4   3   2   1

CONTENTS

Dear Parents,

I wrote the *Before I Dream* Bible stories to be read aloud at bedtime. You can, of course, read them at any time of day. But as I was writing the stories, I remembered nights at the bedsides of my sons when they were young. Sometimes they'd say, "I can't sleep." Or, "When I close my eyes, I have bad dreams." I'd kiss them, stroke their hair, and pray. We'd talk about good memories and happy thoughts that would lead to good dreams.

It was then that I began to realize how important it is to fill our mind with good thoughts before we go to sleep. So I wrote *Before I Dream.*

I tried to fill each story with sights, sounds, textures, smells, and flavors so that as you read, your children will be drawn into the story. They will see, hear, feel, smell, and taste what it might have been like if they had actually been there. I hope these stories will be delightful bedtime treats to nourish your children's hearts and fill their minds with the best of thoughts before they dream.

Many blessings and sweet dreams!
Karyn Henley

OLD TESTAMENT

God's Great Idea

GENESIS 1

Long ago God looked at the dark. It was deep, and it was empty. But God had an idea. "Light!" said God. And light scattered the darkness. Morning came, and then evening—one whole day.

But God did not rest. There was more to his idea. He spread out the wide, wide sky. So there was day and night and wide, wide sky. Two days had passed.

Still, God did not rest. There was more to his idea. He heaped water together to make seas. And he said, "Let's have some dry land with seeds and plants and fruit trees." Day and night, wide, wide sky, water and land with seeds and plants: God saw that it was good. Three days had passed.

But God did not rest. There was more to his idea. "Let's have lights," said God. "A sun, a moon, and twinkling stars." Day and night, wide, wide sky, water and land with seeds and plants, sun and moon and twinkling starlight: God saw that it was good. Four days had passed.

But God did not rest. There was more to his idea. He made swimming water animals. He sent birds flying into the sky. Day and night, wide, wide sky, water and land with seeds and plants, sun and moon and twinkling starlight, animals to swim and fly: God saw that it was good. Five days had passed.

But God did not rest. There was more to his idea. When the sixth day came, he made other animals—runners and jumpers and creepers and crawlers and climbers and divers. Day and night, wide, wide sky, water and land with seeds and plants, sun and moon and

twinkling starlight, animals to swim and fly and run and jump and crawl and climb.

Still, God did not rest. There was more to his idea. "Let's make people," said God. "They can take care of this earth." So God made people much like himself. Day and night, wide, wide sky, water and land with seeds and plants, sun and moon and twinkling starlight, animals to swim and fly and run and jump and crawl and climb, and people much like God himself: God saw that it was all very good. Six days had passed.

And then . . .
God rested.

Rain on the Roof

GENESIS 6–9

Rasp-a-rasp-a-rasp went the saws. *Bam! Bam! Bam! Bam! Bam!*
went the hammers. Noah and his three grown-up boys were
building a boat. A big boat. A gigantic boat for holding all kinds
of animals.

They put a roof on the top of the boat and a door in the side. And then Noah and his big boys brought in all kinds of food for all kinds of animals. And the animals came:

Ducks and horses, cats and dogs,
Owls and chickens, sheep and hogs.

Beavers and chipmunks, squirrels and cows,
Butterflies, zebras, giraffes and—wow—

Beautiful flamingos, the hippopotamus,
Turtles and pandas and waddly platypus,

Tigers and lions and big furry bears,
Rabbits and even armadillos were there,

Robins and peacocks and wiggling monkeys,
Possums and foxes and hee-hawing donkeys,

Huge elephants and teeny-tiny bugs,
Snakes and sparrows and slippery-slimy slugs,

Raccoons and wombats, beetles and bees,
And somebody even brought the fleas!

There were frogs and bugs and kangaroos.
Why, it was beginning to look like a zoo—

And smell like one, too!

Of course, Noah and his wife and their grown-up boys and their wives went into the ark, too. And when everyone was on board and ready to go, God shut the door.

You can imagine the sounds that night as they all tried to go to sleep in that boat together, squawking and grunting and purring and snuffling. But a week later there was another sound—a *pittery-pattery* sound, a *wondery-thundery* sound, and a *swishy-sloshy* sound—as rain began to fall and water began to rise. And that night the boat rocked all the animals to sleep.

For days and days it rained. Even when the rain stopped, the boat kept rocking, because it took days and days for the water to dry up off the ground. But when it did, Noah and his family and all those animals were ready to get out of the boat.

There were animals crawling and creeping, flying and waddling, running and jumping to get off the boat. And when they looked up, they saw a wonderful surprise. There in the sky was a beautiful rainbow to welcome them home.

Count the Stars

GENESIS 15; 18; 21

The leaves of the big oak trees shook in the night breeze. Everything was quiet in the tent nearby. Some people talked softly. Other people were already asleep. Abraham was in his tent, thinking about God.

"Abraham," said God, "don't be afraid. I am taking care of you. I will give you good things."

"But you haven't given me any children," said Abraham.

"Come outside," said God. Abraham stepped outside his tent.

"Now look up at the sky," said God. Abraham looked up at the dark night sky. It was a big wide sky sprinkled with sparkling stars.

"Count the stars if you can," said God.

"There are too many to count!" said Abraham.

"Yes," said God. "But that's how many people will be in your family someday. You will have children. And your children will grow up to have children. And someday your family will be a great nation."

But a long time passed, and Abraham still did not have any children.

One hot day Abraham was sitting at the door of his tent. He looked up and saw three men coming. Abraham went to meet the three men, and he bowed down. "Come and rest under the tree," said Abraham. "I will get you something to eat."

So the men rested under the oak trees while Abraham went into his tent to find his wife, Sarah.

"We have visitors," Abraham told Sarah. "Bake some bread for them."

Then Abraham ran to his servants. "We have visitors," he told them. "Cook some meat for them, and bring some milk."

So Abraham got fresh bread from Sarah. The servants brought meat and milk. And Abraham shared his food with the three visitors.

"Where is Sarah?" asked one of the visitors.

"She's in the tent," said Abraham.

"She will have a baby boy next year," said the man.

Inside the tent, Sarah was listening. When she heard the man say she would have a baby, she laughed. *I'm too old to have a baby,* Sarah thought.

"Why did Sarah laugh?" asked God. "Is anything too hard for the Lord?"

When the visitors got up to leave, Abraham walked down the road with them for a little while.

Abraham thought about what the visitors had said. It reminded him of the night God had showed him the stars. Now God was getting ready to keep his promise. And, yes, the next year God really did give Abraham and Sarah a baby boy!

A Ten-Camel Trip
GENESIS 24

Humpity bumpity, snuffling and snorting, the camels plodded down the road. A servant led ten camels. On their backs were bundles full of all kinds of good things—gold and silver rings and bracelets, clothes, and other beautiful things. These were gifts. But who were they for? No one knew.

The servant was taking these gifts to a young lady somewhere. But he did not know who she was. Abraham had told him to go and find a wife for Isaac, who was Abraham's son. Who would she be? Isaac didn't know. Abraham didn't know. The servant didn't know. But God knew.

Abraham had told his servant, "God will send his angel ahead of you so you can get a wife for Isaac."

So the servant had loaded the camels with the gifts. And now they were on their way, *humpity bumpity,* snuffling and snorting.

The servant and the camels traveled a long way. They finally saw a large city in the distance. The servant was thirsty and ready to rest. The camels were thirsty and ready to rest. So the servant decided to stop just outside the city at a well.

When they stopped at the well, the servant saw that the girls from the city were coming to the well to get water for their families. Would one of these girls be the right wife for Isaac?

The servant prayed, "Oh, Lord God, here I am beside the well. Girls are coming here to get water. I will ask a girl to give me a drink. If she is the one you have chosen to marry Isaac, have her say, 'Here's a drink for you, and I'll give water to your camels, too!'"

Before the servant had finished praying, a beautiful girl came to the well. The servant asked her for a drink. He watched to see if she was the one God had chosen. "Here's a drink for you," she said. "And I'll give water to your camels, too!"

The servant was excited. Here was the girl God had chosen! He gave her a gold ring and two gold bracelets. "What's your name?" he asked.

"I'm Rebekah," she said.

"Is there room at your house for me to spend the night?" asked the servant.

"Yes," said Rebekah. "We even have room for your camels."

Abraham's servant bowed down and worshiped God.

"I praise you, God," he said. "You have led me to the girl you chose for Isaac."

Then the servant went to Rebekah's house. He asked her father if she could marry Isaac.

Rebekah's father said, "Yes."

So the servant opened the camels' packs. Out came the gold and silver rings, the bracelets, the clothes, and the other beautiful things. The servant gave these gifts to Rebekah and her family. Then the servant and his camels spent the night at Rebekah's house.

The next day the servant and Rebekah and the ten camels left to travel back to Abraham and Isaac. *Humpity bumpity,* snuffling and snorting, the camels plodded down the road. They had left all of the expensive gifts behind. But they carried something that was even more important and special. They were bringing Rebekah home to Isaac.

Stairs Full of Angels

GENESIS 28:10-22

The clouds turned gold and orange and pink and red. The sun slowly went down. Stars began to sparkle in the purple evening sky. Jacob knew it was time to find a place to sleep.

Jacob had been walking a long time, and he was tired. He was also all alone. He looked around. There was no bed. There was no pillow. So Jacob chose a stone for a pillow. He put the stone under his head and lay down on the ground to sleep.

While Jacob was asleep that night, he had a dream. In his dream he saw stairs that started on the ground and went up and up and up, all the way to heaven. And on the stairs there were angels, climbing up and down.

God was standing at the very top. He said, "I am the Lord. I am with you. I will watch over you anywhere you go. I will not leave you."

When Jacob woke up, he knew he was not alone after all. "The Lord is here, and I didn't even know it!" he said.

Even in the dark, when nobody else was around, God was there, taking care of him. "This is an awesome place," said Jacob, "because God is here!"

Stars Bow Down

GENESIS 37; 39–45

Oh, it was a beautiful coat! Red and blue and green and yellow! It was like a rainbow. Joseph's father had it made just for him.

But Joseph's brothers didn't like it one bit! They didn't have coats like that. And they were jealous.

One night Joseph had an amazing dream. He saw the sun and the moon and 11 stars. And all of them bowed down to him!

The next day Joseph ran to his father. "Listen to my dream," Joseph said to his father. And he told him his dream. But his father was upset.

"Listen to my dream!" Joseph said to his brothers. And he told them his dream. But they got angry. They wanted to get rid of Joseph. And one day they got their chance.

They were in the fields, taking care of their sheep, when they saw Joseph coming. "Here comes the dreamer!" they said. "We'll take his coat and throw him into a dry well. Then we'll see what happens to all those dreams!" And that's just what they did. Then they sat down to eat their lunch.

While they were eating, they saw a caravan coming. It was a long line of men and their camels. They were going to Egypt.

Joseph's brothers pulled him up out of the well and stopped the men. "Do you want to buy someone to work for you?" they asked.

The men looked at Joseph. And they paid 20 silver coins for him. They took Joseph to Egypt with them, and they sold him.

Joseph had to work very hard. But he did his work the best he could, and he trusted God.

Then one night the king of Egypt had a dream. He dreamed that

seven thin stalks of grain swallowed up seven fat stalks of grain. The king was upset by his strange dream. But no one could tell him what it meant. No one except Joseph.

God told Joseph what the dream meant. And Joseph told the king. For seven years there would be plenty of food. Then for seven years there would not be enough.

The king was pleased that Joseph could tell him about his dream. He made Joseph the ruler of the land. Only the king was greater than Joseph. And Joseph was wise. He saved up food for the hungry years to come.

One day some men from far away came to see Joseph. They all bowed down before him, and they asked him for food. They were Joseph's brothers! Joseph's dream had come true!

Joseph was kind to his brothers. He said, "You meant to hurt me. But God made it all turn out to be good."

The Basket-Bed

EXODUS 2:1-10

"This is a fine baby boy!" said the mother. She snuggled him close. She was hiding him from the mean king who wanted to kill all the boy babies.

This baby was small. But he grew bigger every day. He began to make loud baby noises. And the mother could not keep him quiet.

She knew the mean king would find him. So she got a special basket with a cover on the top. Then she put tar on the bottom and up the sides so water could not get in. This basket would be a boat. It would be a bed for her baby.

She wrapped the baby snug and warm. And she gently put him in the basket-bed. Then the mother and the baby's big sister walked to the wide river. They waded through the tall water plants. And they set the basket-boat down on top of the water.

The water swished this way. The water sloshed that way. And it rocked the baby in his basket-bed.

The mother walked home. But the sister stayed by the river. She hid behind the tall water plants. And she watched the little basket-boat float at the side of the river.

Soon she heard some people talking. It was the princess and her servant girls. They were coming very close to the place where the basket-bed was.

The princess looked at the water. And she pointed. She was looking at the basket!

A servant girl waded over to the basket. She pulled it back with her and took it to the princess. The princess opened it.

"It's a baby!" said the princess. The baby began to cry. The princess felt sorry for him. "Oh!" said the princess. "I love this baby. I will keep him, and he'll be my baby! I will name him Moses!"

The baby's sister was brave. She ran right up to the princess. "I could get somebody to take care of your baby for you. Just until he grows big enough to come and live with you."

"Yes!" said the princess. "That's a good idea!"

So the baby's sister ran home. She came back with her own mother—the baby's mother! And the princess let her take the baby home. So the mother got her own baby back!

"He's a fine baby!" said the mother. "He's a wonderful baby!" She snuggled him close. She didn't have to hide him anymore.

And when he grew big enough, she took him to live in the palace with the princess!

Let Us Go!

EXODUS 7–12

Plop went the muddy clay. Then into the clay went the straw: *Slop! Plop, slop, mix, mix, mix.* God's people were making bricks. They worked and worked, harder and harder, making bricks for the mean king so he could build his cities.

"Help us, God!" the people cried. "Save us from this mean king!"

God heard his people praying. He saw how badly the king treated them. So God sent Moses to talk to the king.

"God says you must let his people go and worship him in the desert," said Moses.

"No," said the king.

So God spoiled their water. The king's people couldn't drink it.

But still the king said, "No. God's people cannot go."

So hopping, croaking, slimy frogs came up from the river and covered the land. *Hop, hop, hop,* they hopped into the houses. *Hop, hop, hop,* they hopped into ovens! *Hop, hop, hop,* they hopped into bowls!

"Go!" said the king. "Pray that God will take the frogs away. Then go!" But then the king thought about it. And the king said, "No! God's people cannot go!"

Then, tiny as dust, filling the air, nipping gnats swarmed everywhere.

But the king said, "No! God's people cannot go!"

Then, black and buzzing, flies flew in, covering the ground where the king's people lived. But the flies didn't go where God's people lived. God took care of his people.

Still, the king said, "No! God's people cannot go!"

So the animals that belonged to the king's people got sick. Then even the king's *people* got sick. But not God's people. God took care of his people.

Still, the king said, "No! God's people cannot go!"

Then *clink, clink, clankety clunk,* down from the sky came ice in chunks. Hail fell all over the king's land, but not on God's people. God took care of his people.

Still, the king said, "No! God's people cannot go!"

So God sent fluttering, flitting, chomping, chewing grasshoppers. They ate the plants that the king's people had planted. But not the plants that belonged to God's people. God took care of his people.

Still, the king said, "No! God's people cannot go!"

Then God sent deep, deep darkness to cover the king's land. But not the place where God's people lived. God took care of his people.

Still, the king said, "No! God's people cannot go."

So the oldest boys in the king's land died. But not the boys of God's people. God took care of his people.

Then the king said, "Yes! God's people can go!"

So out went the boys, and out went the girls. Out went the women and men and babies. Out went their cows and sheep and donkeys, *rattledy, rattledy,* pulling their wagons.

God's people left the land of Egypt.

God took care of his people.

A Night-Light in the Clouds

EXODUS 13:21–14:31

Clippety-clop! Clinkety-clink! Rumbledy-rumbledy-bump! Over the ground they came—carts and cows and sheep, mothers and dads, grandmas and grandpas, boys and girls. They were God's people. Walking and riding, away from Egypt they came, away from the mean king.

God was leading them. In the daytime God went in front of them in a big tall cloud. If they followed the cloud, they would know which way to go. At night the cloud was filled with fire. It would shine down all through the night. So they could travel in the daytime or at night.

At first the cloud led them by the desert. No one lived there. Then the cloud led them to the Red Sea. It was big and deep.

One day the people saw some people coming toward them across the land. It was the mean king and his army! He was coming after them to catch them and take them back to Egypt! They were scared! They prayed to God!

Moses was leading God's people. He said, "God will fight for you. All you need to do is be still."

And God did fight for them. God's angel had been traveling in front of the people. Now he moved behind them. And the tall cloud moved behind them, too. The angel and the cloud came between the mean king's army and God's people.

That night the cloud made it dark on the side where the army was. And the cloud made it light on the side where God's people were.

God told Moses to hold out his hand over the sea. So Moses did. Then God sent a strong wind from the east. It blew all night and pushed the sea back so that it made two walls of water with a dry road in between.

God's people crossed the sea on that dry road. But when the mean king's army tried to follow, the water splashed back down all over the army.

God's people saw his great power. They thanked God and praised him.

God kept leading his people in the cloud during the day. And at night he filled the cloud with light so they could see. It reminded them that God was watching over them.

Surprises to Eat

EXODUS 16:1-17, 31, 35

Clip-clop-clip went the donkeys. *Trip-trot-trip* went the sheep. *Rattle-rattle-bump* went the carts. *Step, step, step* went the people. Walking, walking, walking. God's people went through the desert. Moms and dads, grandpas and grandmas, aunts and uncles and cousins, girls and boys.

Moses was leading them. They were walking away from Egypt, where the mean king had made them do hard work. They were walking to a new place. It had rivers and fields, gardens and lakes.

But first they had to go through the desert. Sometimes it was hard to find water. Sometimes it was hard to find food. Then the people complained to Moses. "We miss all the good food we ate in Egypt," they said.

God heard what they said. And God told Moses, "I am going to give you food. Then everyone will know that I am the Lord your God."

That evening, as the sun began to go down, the first part of God's surprise came. The people looked out from their tents. They saw lots of little birds coming. More and more came. And they landed in the camp. They were quail birds.

That night the people had quail meat for dinner. And when they went to bed, they weren't hungry anymore.

Early the next morning, while the people were asleep, the second part of God's surprise came. Dew appeared on the ground. When the people woke up, they saw the dew. But when the dew dried up, something special happened. The dew left something behind. It was white. And it looked like frost. But it wasn't.

Moses said, "This is bread from God. Take as much as you need."

So the people picked up the special bread. And they ate it for breakfast. It tasted like honey cakes. The people called the special bread *manna*.

And God kept giving them this special bread as long as they were traveling, because God loves his people and takes care of them.

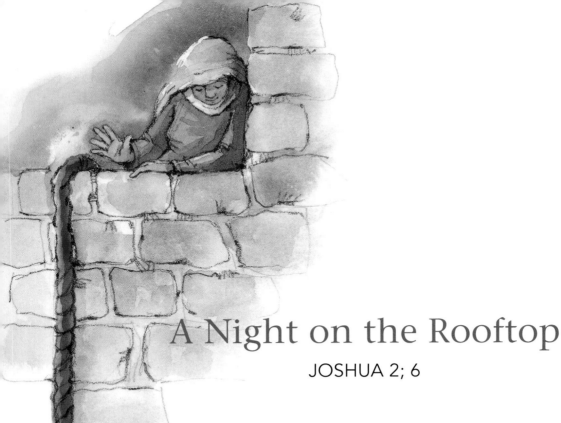

A Night on the Rooftop

JOSHUA 2; 6

The sun had gone down. The sky was getting darker and darker. The stars were growing bright and twinkly. Once in a while a cloud would hide the moon. And up on Rahab's rooftop, two men were hiding.

Behind the water pot? No.

By the wall at the top of the stairs? No.

Under the piles of flax plants drying on the roof? Yes. That's where Rahab had told the men to hide. These men were two of God's people. They were spies who had come to see what the strange city of Jericho was like.

As the spies hid, still and quiet under piles of flax, they could hear voices in the house below. People were talking and laughing in Rahab's house. Dishes rattled and jars clinked.

Then a *knock, knock, knock* came on the door. Some deep voices talked. "Bring out the spies who are here at your house," said the voices. The voices belonged to men sent from the king to catch the spies.

But the spies heard Rahab say, "Two men did come. Then they left again just as the sun was going down. If you hurry, you might catch them."

The spies heard the footsteps of the men running down the road, getting farther and farther away. They heard the *thump* of Rahab's door closing. They heard the *clank* of the latch locking the door.

Then *step, step, step,* Rahab came up the stairs to the roof. "You can come out now," she said. "But before you go to sleep on my roof, I want to ask you something. I believe in God. I know that God will give this city to you and your people. Since I have helped you, will you save me and my family?"

The spies nodded. "Yes," they said, "if you will promise not to tell anyone what we were doing here."

"I promise," said Rahab.

Now Rahab's house was built into part of the thick wall around the city. So Rahab let the spies get away by having them climb down a rope from her window.

"Leave this red rope in your window," the spies told her. "Then our people will know that everyone in your house is to be saved."

So Rahab let the red rope hang out her window. When God's people marched around the city of Jericho, they saw the red rope hanging there.

Rahab watched them march around, tramping, tramping. She heard their horns blow: *Ta-ra! Ta-ra!* She heard God's people shout loudly! Suddenly the walls around the city began to shake and fall.

But did Rahab's part of the wall fall? No. God kept Rahab safe.

Then the two spies went to Rahab's house. They got everyone in her family out safely. After that, Rahab and her family became God's people, too.

Sun and Moon, Stand Still!

JOSHUA 10:1-15

Five kings came marching, marching, marching. Their armies came marching, marching behind them. They marched to the city of Gibeon and lined up to fight.

The people of Gibeon saw the kings and their armies, and they were afraid. They sent a message to Joshua, the leader of God's people. "Help!" said the message. "Come and save us!"

So Joshua called his army together. All the best fighting men from God's people were in this army.

"Don't be afraid," God told Joshua. "You will win."

Now it was nighttime. But Joshua and his men marched out toward Gibeon. They came marching, marching all night long.

When the sun came up the next morning, the five kings woke up to see Joshua and his army. He had come to save the people of Gibeon.

Joshua and his army surprised the five kings and their armies. He won a big fight. Then the other armies began running away. But God sent big hailstones pinging, pounding from the sky to stop them.

This fighting and running lasted all day. The sun began to get lower in the sky. Joshua could see that the sky would be dark before the fighting was finished. So Joshua asked God to help.

"Oh, God, let the sun stand still over Gibeon," said Joshua. "Oh, God, let the moon stand still over the valley."

The bright, hot sun stopped crossing the sky. It beamed down steadily, and the day grew longer. The curved white moon stopped right where it was. Both the sun and the moon stopped for a whole day until God's people won the fight!

And there has never been a day like that before or since!

Wet Wool

JUDGES 6:34–7:9, 16-22

Ta-da, went the trumpet. *Ta-da! Ta-da! Ta-da!*

Many men heard the trumpet sound. And they came. Gideon was blowing his trumpet. He was calling God's men to come out and fight the enemies. *Ta-da! Ta-da! Ta-da!* The men came. And they got ready.

But Gideon wanted to be sure that God would help them. So that night, he prayed. "Oh, God, I want to know if you will save us. So I will put some sheep's wool on the ground tonight. The cool, wet, night dew will come. In the morning I will look at the wool. If the dew is on the wool but the ground is dry, then I will know you will save us."

So Gideon put the sheep's wool on the ground. And then he went to bed.

Early in the morning Gideon got up. The ground was dry. But the sheep's wool was wet with dew. It was so wet that Gideon squeezed a whole bowl full of water out of it!

But Gideon wanted to be very, very sure. He prayed again. "Oh, God, let me check this one more time. Tonight, keep the wool dry. But make the ground get wet with dew."

That night Gideon set the wool on the ground. Then he went to bed.

Early the next morning Gideon got up. And he went to look at the wool. It was dry, but the ground was wet with dew! So Gideon knew that God would be with him.

That night, in the middle of the night, God told Gideon, "It's time. You must go to the enemy camp now!"

So Gideon took his men with him. He gave each man a trumpet and a jar with a fiery torch inside. And Gideon said, "Watch me! Do exactly what I do!"

It was still late in the night. And it was very dark. Gideon and his men crept down to the enemy camp. They all made a big circle and stood around the camp. The enemies were sleeping.

All at once Gideon blew his trumpet and smashed his jar! His men blew their trumpets! They smashed their jars! And they yelled, "A sword for the Lord and for Gideon!"

The fiery torches lit up the camp. All this noise and light woke the enemies up. And it scared them. They thought a huge army was after them. So God had them begin fighting each other. Then they ran away.

God had kept his promise. He had saved Gideon and his friends.

The Riddle

JUDGES 14:5-19

Down the road walked Samson—
down the road toward the
town of Timnah. All of a
sudden a lion leaped out
from behind some big rocks.
Growling and roaring, the
lion ran toward Samson.
Then it jumped at Samson!
Samson grabbed the
lion's thick, hairy hide. He
fought the lion with his bare
hands and killed it!

God had made Samson
strong so that Samson could
save his people. God had told
Samson's mother never to cut
her son's hair. So Samson wore
his long, long hair in seven braids.
As long as Samson obeyed God, he
was strong.

After Samson killed the lion, he
went on to town. But he didn't tell
anyone about the lion.

Some time later Samson walked
to Timnah again. He stopped at the

place where he had killed the lion. The bones of the lion were still lying there. And buzzing in and out and all around were bees. They had made a nest among the lion's bones, and there was honey inside!

Samson scooped up some of the golden, sweet honey. He ate it as he walked to town.

In town Samson went to a party. The girl Samson was going to marry was there. Thirty young men were also at the party.

"I have a riddle for you," Samson told the young men. "Out of the eater came something to eat. Out of the strong came something sweet. I'll give you one week to find the answer to my riddle. If you find the answer, I will give each of you a set of clothes. If you don't find the answer, each of you must give me a set of clothes."

One day passed. The young men thought and thought.

Two days passed. They thought and thought some more.

Three days passed. Still the young men didn't know the answer.

The young men began to get worried on the fourth day. "This isn't fair," they told Samson's girlfriend. "Get Samson to tell you what the riddle is about."

So Samson's girlfriend went to him, and she cried. "You don't love me," she said. "You didn't tell me the answer to the riddle."

"I didn't even tell my mother and father," said Samson. "Why should I tell you?"

Samson's girlfriend cried every day and said, "Tell me the answer to the riddle."

Five days passed. Then six days. At last, on the seventh day, Samson told his girlfriend the answer to the riddle.

Right away Samson's girlfriend went to the young men and told them the answer to the riddle.

That afternoon, before the sun went down, the young men went to Samson. "We know the answer to the riddle!" they said. "The sweet is honey, and the strong is a lion!"

Samson knew they had not thought of the answer by themselves. "You would never have learned the answer if my girlfriend hadn't told you!" said Samson.

Samson was angry, but he kept his promise. He gave each young man a set of clothes. And he did not marry his girlfriend. Instead, he went home to his father and mother's house.

Gathering Grain

RUTH

Naomi shaded her eyes from the sun. She looked down the road. It stretched across the fields of Moab. Then it went over a hill, out of sight.

Naomi would have to walk down this long road to get back to her old home in Bethlehem. Naomi's husband had died in Moab. Her two grown sons had died. Now Naomi had only two people left in her family: Ruth and Orpah, the women her sons had married.

"You two should stay here in Moab," Naomi told them. "Go live with your father and mother now."

So Orpah hugged Naomi and told her good-bye.

But Ruth said, "Don't ask me to leave you. I want to go where you go. I want your people to be my people. I want your God to be my God."

So Naomi and Ruth picked up their bags. Step by step they started down the long dirt road.

When Naomi and Ruth got to Bethlehem, they needed food. Ruth said, "I know! I'll go to the fields where people are gathering grain. I'll pick up the grain that's left over."

So Ruth found a field to work in. She followed the farm workers all morning long, their feet shuffling, shuffling, as they walked through the grain field. Their long, curved harvesting knives swished this way and that as they cut down the tall stalks of grain. *Bunch, bunch, bunch,* they bundled the grain together. *Shuffle, shuffle, swish, swish, bunch, bunch, bunch.*

Ruth watched for some of the grain to fall out of the bundles. She picked it up.

Bunch, bunch, bunch. She made a small bundle of her own.

In a little while Boaz came to watch his workers. "God be with you!" he called to his workers.

"God be with you!" they called back to Boaz.

Then Boaz saw Ruth. "Who is that?" Boaz asked the man in charge.

"That's the woman who came back with Naomi," the man answered.

Boaz walked over to Ruth. "Welcome to my field," he told her. "Stay close to my servant girls and you will be safe. When you get thirsty, drink from our water jars."

"You are very kind to me," said Ruth.

"I heard how you left your home so you could come and help Naomi," said Boaz. "God will bless you for that."

When it was lunchtime, Boaz asked Ruth to come and eat with him. And when Ruth went back to the field, Boaz told his workers to pull grain from their bundles and drop it behind on the ground for Ruth to pick up.

Ruth took lots of grain home that day.

"Where did you work?" asked Naomi.

"I worked in Boaz's field," said Ruth.

"God bless Boaz!" said Naomi. "God is doing something wonderful here!"

God *was* doing something wonderful,

because Boaz and Ruth liked each other very much. It wasn't long until they got married. And some time later they had a baby boy.

Naomi held the baby and helped take care of him. Now she had a new family. She was glad she had made the long trip home.

Who's Calling?

1 SAMUEL 3

Eli took care of the house of worship. But Eli was old. His eyes could hardly see. So Eli had a helper, a boy named Samuel. The boy loved God and obeyed Eli. At night the man and the boy each had a place to sleep right there in the house of worship.

Now the sun had gone down one evening. The lamp was still shining inside. But Eli had already gone to bed. Samuel lay down on his bed, too.

Soft night sounds were all around. The wind whispered. Night bugs chirped. A dog yapped at the moon. And then the boy heard, "Samuel!"

Samuel was the helper, so he got up and ran to Eli. "Here I am," Samuel said. "You called me."

But Eli said, "I didn't call you. Go back to bed."

So Samuel went back to bed. The wind whispered. Night bugs buzzed. An owl hooted. And then he heard it again. "Samuel! Samuel!"

Samuel got up and ran to Eli. "I'm right here," Samuel said. "You called me."

But Eli said, "I didn't call you. Go back to bed."

So Samuel went back to bed. The wind whispered. Night bugs hummed. A little mouse rustled the grass outside. And then he heard it again. "Samuel! Samuel!"

Samuel got up and ran to Eli. "I'm right here," he said. "You called me."

Then Eli understood what was happening. God had been calling Samuel! So Eli said, "Go back to bed. If you hear someone calling again, say, 'I'm listening, Lord.'"

Samuel went back to bed. The wind whispered. Night bugs whirred. A sheep baaed out in the field. Then he heard it again. "Samuel! Samuel!"

Samuel said, "I'm listening, Lord."

So God told Samuel that he was not going to let Eli's two sons work at the house of worship anymore. It was because they did not love God. And they did not obey Eli. Then God was quiet.

The wind whispered. The night bugs flitted. Eli snored. And Samuel knew that he was not alone. Even though God was quiet, God was there, taking care of him.

Lost Donkeys and a King

1 SAMUEL 9–10

Maybe someone forgot to watch the donkeys. Maybe someone left the gate open. Maybe the donkeys just pushed the gate open. However it happened, the donkeys wandered away from their farm.

Saul's father came and told him the news. "Our donkeys are lost," he said. "Take a servant with you, and go look for them."

So Saul and his servant went looking for the donkeys. They looked through the grasses and groves. But no donkeys. They looked along the rocky hillsides. But no donkeys. They looked beside rivers and streams. But no donkeys.

Saul and his servant looked for three days and never found the donkeys. Finally Saul said, "Let's go back home. Now my father will start worrying about *us* instead of the donkeys."

But the servant said, "Let's go see Samuel, the man of God. Maybe he can tell us where the donkeys are."

"Good idea," said Saul.

So Saul and his servant went to the town where Samuel lived. Now, Saul had never seen Samuel before. So he asked a man, "Can you please tell me where Samuel's house is?"

"I'm Samuel," said the man. "And I'm having a dinner party. I want you to come and eat with me. By the way, don't worry about those donkeys that were lost. Your father has found them."

Saul was surprised. But he and his servant went with Samuel. They went to a big house and sat at a long table with 30 other people. The cook brought dinner, and they all ate.

By the time dinner was over, it was getting dark. So Saul and his servant went to Samuel's house to spend the night. Samuel went with Saul up to the roof of the house. They talked together under the stars.

The next morning they got up very early. Samuel walked with Saul and his servant to the edge of town. Then Samuel poured some oil on Saul's head. "You will be the first king of God's people," said Samuel.

Saul went back home. He didn't tell anyone what Samuel had said.

But one day it was time to crown the new king. All the people got together with Samuel.

"Where is Saul?" asked Samuel.

"Where is Saul?" asked the old men and women.

"Where is Saul?" asked the young men and women.

"Where is Saul?" asked the children.

The people looked and looked for Saul. At last someone found him. He was hiding behind some boxes and bags. The people brought Saul to Samuel.

"This is the man God has chosen to be your king," said Samuel.

"Hurrah!" shouted the people. "Long live the king! Long live the king! Long live Saul our king!"

The Harp Player
1 SAMUEL 16:1-13, 23; PSALM 63:6-8, 11

The little sheep baaed and baaed. Its wool was caught in the thorny bushes.

David pushed the bushes aside with his shepherd's staff. He tapped the little sheep so it would move out of the brambles. Soon it was free of the thorny branches, and it bounded off to join the rest of the sheep. Silly sheep! David laughed.

At last all the sheep were lazily nibbling at the green grass. It was a big job to watch the sheep by yourself. But David's father and his big brothers had gone to eat dinner with the people from town. *The prophet Samuel, a man who told about God, will be at the dinner, too. So it must be important,* thought David.

David was glad to stay behind with the sheep. He liked being outdoors. He liked to talk to God out there in the fields. And it was a good time to play his harp.

David sat down under a tree and began to play some music. He sang a song to God while he watched his sheep.

Then David heard somebody calling him.

"David! David!" It was one of his family's servants. "The prophet Samuel is asking for you," he said. "He says they won't eat until you get there."

"They're waiting for me?" said David.

The servant nodded.

David stood up and took a quick look around to make sure all

the sheep were there. Some were still nibbling grass. Some were dozing. Some were drinking water from a little stream. But they were all there.

David handed his shepherd's staff to the servant. Then he hurried down the path to town.

Sure enough, everyone was waiting for David. There was his father. There were his big brothers. And there was Samuel the prophet, the man of God.

Samuel walked over to David. David bowed his head, and Samuel poured oil onto David's head. Then David knew that this was a very important dinner. The oil meant that God had chosen David. Someday David would be the new king for God's people.

For now there was already a king. His name was Saul. David would wait until it was his turn to be king. Until then, he played his harp and watched the sheep and sang songs to God. He even played his harp and sang for King Saul!

David loved music. One of his songs said,

I lie awake and think of you, God.
I think of you through the night.
I think about how you have helped me.
I sing because you take care of me.
Your right hand is strong.
You hold me safely.
So I will sing for joy.

Fighting the Giant

1 SAMUEL 17–18:5

Ten loaves of brown bread. Ten big chunks of smooth cheese. A half bushel of crunchy roasted grain. These were gifts for the captain of King Saul's army. David bundled the bread and cheese and grain together.

Three of David's brothers were soldiers in the king's army. David's father wanted to find out how they were doing. So he had asked David to take these gifts to the captain.

David left his sheep with another shepherd, and down the road he went with the pack of gifts. Down the road, across the field, over hill and valley, hill and valley, hill and valley.

At last David could see two armies in the distance. An enemy army was camped on one hill. King Saul's army was camped on another hill. There was a valley between the two camps. David hurried to King Saul's camp.

Just as David got to the camp, a giant man over nine feet tall came down the hill from the enemy camp. This giant wore a big helmet. He carried a huge spear. And he shouted to King Saul's army, "Send somebody to fight me!"

The soldiers in King Saul's army stepped back. Some ran to hide. "Do you see that giant, Goliath?" they asked David. "Every day he comes out yelling at us!"

"How can you let this giant stand against God?" asked David. He went to King Saul's tent. "I'll go fight Goliath," David told the king.

"You're just a boy," said King Saul. "How could you possibly fight a giant?"

"When lions and bears came after my sheep, I fought them and killed them," said David. "And that's what I'll do to this giant!"

David went to the bubbling stream nearby. He reached into the clear, cold water and picked out five smooth stones. David put the stones in his bag. Then he walked down the hill and across the valley toward the giant.

"Ha!" shouted Goliath when he saw David coming. "Do you think I'm a dog that you can beat with a stick? Come here, and I'll feed you to the wild animals!"

But David did not step back like the other soldiers did. He did not run and hide. Instead, David shouted back at the giant. "You come against me with a spear and a sword. But I come against you in the name of the Lord! God doesn't need swords to win a fight, and this fight belongs to God! Today God will win!"

Goliath started coming toward David. But David was fast. He put one of the smooth stones into his sling. He whirled the sling around and around. *Whirrr!*

Suddenly the stone shot out, zipped through the air, and hit Goliath in the forehead. Goliath swayed and staggered and fell facedown.

When the enemy army saw that their champion was dead, they were the ones who turned and ran away! And after that, David became a mighty warrior in Saul's army.

The King's Dream

1 KINGS 3:3-15; 2 CHRONICLES 1; 9

Solomon was the king of God's people. He had a crown and a throne, and he was building a new palace. But he had not been king very long. His father David had been the king before. David had loved and obeyed God. He had been a good king. Now it was Solomon's turn. Solomon had decided that he would love and obey God too.

One day Solomon went to worship God at a special place called Gibeon. That night God came to Solomon in a dream.

God said, "Solomon, you may ask me for anything you want."

Solomon said, "You have been very kind to my father, and now you are letting me be the king. But I feel like a little child. I don't really know how to be king. What I really want is a wise heart so I can be a good king. I want a wise heart so I can tell what is right and what is wrong."

God was very glad that Solomon had asked for a wise heart. God said, "You did not ask for a long life or lots of money. You did not even ask me to get rid of your enemies. Instead, you asked me for a wise heart. So I will give you a wise heart. I will help you understand what is right and what is wrong just as you asked. You will be the wisest man who ever lived."

Then God said, "I will also give you some things you did not ask for. You will be very rich. And if you love and obey me, I will give you a long life, too."

When Solomon woke up, he went back to Jerusalem and thanked God. Then he had a great party for all his friends and helpers.

God made Solomon so wise that every year many people came

to hear what he had to say. And when they came, they brought Solomon gold and silver, robes and sweet-smelling spices, horses and donkeys. So Solomon became very rich, just like God had promised.

King Solomon had a throne made of ivory and gold. There were six steps up to the throne, with twelve lion statues on the steps and one lion statue on each side of the throne. All of King Solomon's cups and dishes were made of gold. King Solomon's ships sailed far and near, bringing back gold and silver and ivory and apes and baboons.

But King Solomon's most important treasure was the wisdom God gave him because he had asked for it in his dream.

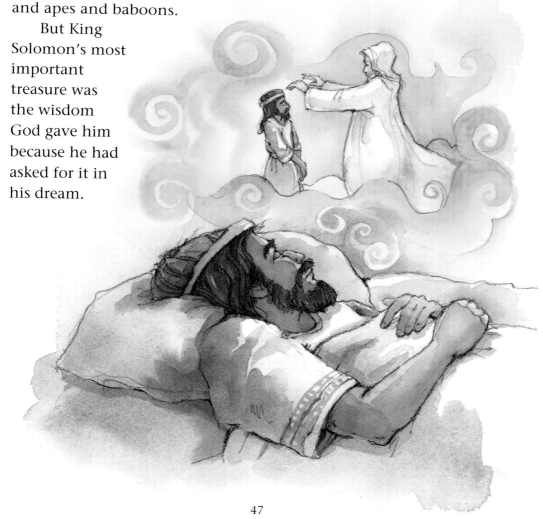

Bread and Meat, Flour and Oil

1 KINGS 17:1-16

It hadn't rained in a long time. People watched the sky. But no rain came. The wind blew. But no rain came. Clouds floated by. But no rain came.

Without rain, fruits and vegetables didn't grow. People were running out of food. Without rain, grass didn't grow. Cows and horses and donkeys and sheep were running out of food. Without rain, rivers and streams began drying up. Soon there would be no water to use for washing and no water to drink.

It was all King Ahab's fault. He did not worship God. Instead, he built idols and worshiped these false gods. So God sent Elijah to tell King Ahab that it would not rain for a long time. That's why the land was drying up.

Elijah loved and obeyed God, but he lived in this land, too. Where would he get water? Where would he get food? And where would he hide from the angry king?

God told Elijah, "Go and hide at Kerith Brook."

So that's where Elijah went. Every morning and every evening birds brought him bread and meat. And Elijah drank water out of the brook.

But day after day went by without any rain. The brook turned into a small stream. Then it became just a trickle of water. Finally it dried up.

God told Elijah, "Go to the town near Sidon. I have told a lady there to share her food with you."

So Elijah walked toward the city of Sidon. When he came to the town nearby, he saw a woman picking up sticks. "Would you please bring me some water?" Elijah asked.

"All right," said the woman, turning to go and get water.

"Bring me some bread, too," said Elijah.

But the woman said, "I don't have any bread. I have only a bit of flour in my flour jar and a bit of oil in my oil jar. You see, I was just getting these sticks to build a small fire so I could cook. I'm going to make some bread for me and my son to eat for supper. But then the oil and flour will be gone, and we will have no more food."

"Bake me some bread first," said Elijah. "And don't be afraid. You will have plenty of flour and plenty of oil to make supper every night until God sends rain. Then the crops will grow again, and there will be food to eat."

So the woman baked bread for Elijah. When she was done, she still had enough flour and oil to make supper for herself and her son.

Every day Elijah ate with the woman and her son. They never ran out of flour and oil. And they never had to go to bed hungry. God always made sure that the woman who shared had enough to eat!

Upstairs

2 KINGS 4:8-11

Step, step, up the stairs, up the stairs went the rich lady. *Step, step,* up the stairs, up the stairs went her husband. They went all the way up, up, up, up to the roof of their house. The roof was flat. It was a good place to look at the stars.

"Here is the place," said the lady. "Here is where we can build a small room for Elisha, the man of God. He comes to our town a lot. If we make a small room for him, he will have a place to stay whenever he comes here. We will put a bed in the room—and a table and a chair and a lamp."

So, *step, step,* up the stairs, up the stairs went the workers. *Step, step,* up the stairs they carried the clay bricks and tools. Then they piled up the bricks and stuck them together to make the walls. They made the corners. They made the windows and the door.

When the room was built, *step, step,* up the stairs, up the stairs they carried the bed. *Step, step,* up the stairs, up the stairs they carried the table. *Step, step,* up the stairs, up the stairs they carried the chair. *Step, step,* up the stairs, up the stairs they carried the lamp. Soon the room was ready.

The next time Elisha came to town, the lady asked him to come to her house. Then she and her husband showed Elisha the surprise! *Step, step,* up the stairs, up the stairs they went.

"Here it is," said the lady. She showed Elisha the small room.

Elisha went in and saw the bed and the table. He saw the chair and the lamp.

"We built it for you," the lady said.

It was just right. Whenever Elisha came to town, he stayed in the room upstairs. It was a good place to sleep.

And when Elisha was not sleepy, he could walk out the door onto the flat roof. It was a good place to look at the stars.

Washing in the River

2 KINGS 5:1-19

The servant girl made the bed. She cleared away the dirty dishes. She brought drinks. She laid out the mirror, the comb, and the brush. She smoothed the wrinkles out of the fancy robes. She was one of God's people. And she worked for the wife of Captain Naaman in the land of Aram.

The servant girl felt sorry for Captain Naaman because he had very bad sores on his skin. So one day she told Naaman's wife about Elisha, a man of God. "Elisha could make the captain well again," the girl said.

Captain Naaman's wife told him about Elisha. They wondered, *Could this be true? Could Elisha really make Captain Naaman well?*

Naaman called for his men, his horses, and his chariots. He packed silver and gold and clothes as gifts. Then Captain Naaman and his men galloped off to see Elisha.

Down the road they went, Naaman and his men. They rode up to Elisha's door. They knocked and waited.

But Elisha didn't come. Instead, he sent a servant to the door with a message for Naaman. "Elisha says you should go to the Jordan River," said the servant. "Wash yourself in the river seven times. Then you will be well again."

Captain Naaman frowned. "Elisha didn't even come out to see me!" he said angrily. "I wanted him to wave his hand over me and make me well. We have rivers in our own country that are better than all the rivers of your country. Why can't I wash in our rivers to get well?"

But Naaman's men said, "Did Elisha ask you to do something hard? All he said was to wash in the Jordan River. Shouldn't you at least try it?"

So Captain Naaman and his men got back on their horses and back in their chariots. They made their horses gallop off to the Jordan River.

Splash! Drip, drip, drip. Captain Naaman dipped into the river one time. He was still sick.

Splash! Drip, drip, drip. He dipped into the river a second time. He was still sick.

Splash, drip, splash, drip, splash, drip, splash, drip. Three, four, five, six times he dipped into the river. He was still sick.

Splash, drip. When Naaman came out of the water after the seventh time, his skin was as clear and clean as a child's skin! He was well!

Captain Naaman and his men hurried back to find Elisha. "Now I know that your God is the real God," said Naaman.

Captain Naaman tried to give Elisha the gifts of gold and silver and clothes. But Elisha would not take them.

"Go home in peace," Elisha told Naaman.

And Naaman did!

Singing instead of Fighting
2 CHRONICLES 20

All the men came. All the women came. All the big children and the little ones came. Even King Jehoshaphat came. They all came and stood together to pray because they were scared. A mighty enemy army was coming to fight them.

King Jehoshaphat stood up in front of everyone, and he led the prayer. "Oh, Lord God," he prayed. "You are the king over all the earth. You are powerful and mighty. But the enemy army is coming to fight us. We are not strong enough to win the fight. We don't know what to do. So we are looking for your help."

Then God said, "Don't be afraid. This is my fight. Tomorrow you must march out to the valley to fight the enemy. But I will be with you."

Then King Jehoshaphat and all the men, all the women, all the big children, and all the little ones bowed down and worshiped God.

Early the next morning the men lined up so they could march out to the valley where the enemy army was. The first people in line were the singers. *Tramp, tramp, tramp.* They led everyone out to the valley as they sang, "Thank God! Thank God! His love lasts forever!"

Tramp, tramp, tramp, marching and singing they came. And as they came, God made the enemy army get all mixed up. They began to fight each other! Swords clashed and shields bashed. The enemy soldiers fought and yelled and chased each other away.

So when King Jehoshaphat's army got to the valley, his men just stood there looking around in amazement. God had already won the

fight! So they sang even louder and praised God. They called that
place the Valley of Praise.

Then God's people turned around and *tramp, tramp,* they
marched back home. They took their harps and trumpets to the
worship house. There all the men, all the women, all the big children
and the little ones—and even King Jehoshaphat—thanked and
praised God!

The Broken Wall

NEHEMIAH 1–3; 8:9-12

Clear red wine had been poured into a big silver cup. Nehemiah carried it to the king of Persia.

The king took the cup of wine. And he looked at Nehemiah. "Why are you sad?" asked the king. "You are not sick, are you? Your heart must be sad."

Nehemiah had worked for the king for a long time. But the king had never seen him look sad before.

"I am sad because I had some bad news," said Nehemiah. "Some friends came to see me. They are from the country where I grew up. They are from Jerusalem, my hometown. And they told me that the city is all broken down. Enemies broke down the walls and burned the gates. It makes me sad just to think about it."

"What can I do for you?" asked the king.

Nehemiah prayed. Then he said, "Let me go back to my old country. Let me help build up the city walls around Jerusalem."

The king let Nehemiah go, even sending a letter to the keeper of the king's forest. The letter told the forest keeper to give Nehemiah

some wood for the walls and the gates. It also said to give Nehemiah wood to make a house for himself.

So Nehemiah went back to Jerusalem.

One night, while everyone else was asleep, Nehemiah got on his horse. And he rode out through the Valley Gate.

Nehemiah rode around the walls. He looked at them very carefully.

They were broken down. And some of the gates had been burned. He rode to the Fountain Gate. He rode to the King's Pool. And then he went up the valley.

As he was riding, Nehemiah looked carefully at the places that needed to be fixed. No one knew where he was or what he was doing because he went in the middle of the night. And everyone was asleep.

The next day Nehemiah told the people, "We have a problem. The walls need to be built up again. Come on and help me build them up."

So they did. The people worked hard. They hammered. *Pound! Pound!* They sawed. *Rizz! Razz!*

Up and up and up the wall went—until one day the whole wall around the city of Jerusalem was built back up. Then people came back to live there.

Nehemiah told the people to have a party! "Be happy!" said Nehemiah. "For the Lord's joy makes you strong!"

The King Who Could Not Sleep

ESTHER 1–6

King Xerxes was very powerful. Whatever he said was the law. King Xerxes had a queen named Esther. She was one of God's people, but the king didn't know it.

Esther's cousin Mordecai often sat at the king's gate. From there he could hear news about Esther. One day Mordecai heard two guards talking. They were making plans to kill the king. Mordecai told Queen Esther, and she told the king. So the king got rid of those two guards. Mordecai had saved the king's life. And the whole story was written down in the king's book.

Now there was an important man in the kingdom named Haman. He was very proud. And he didn't like Mordecai because this man wouldn't bow down to him. So Haman decided to get rid of Mordecai.

One night Haman went to see the king. He wanted to talk about how he could kill Mordecai. He waited out in the halls so he could see the king as soon as possible.

That night the king couldn't sleep. So he asked a servant to read aloud from his book. The servant read the part that told how Mordecai had saved the king's life.

"How did we thank Mordecai?" asked the king.

"We didn't thank him," said the servant.

"Who is out in my halls right now?" asked the king.

The servant told the king that Haman was out there.

"Bring Haman in here," ordered the king.

So Haman came in.

"There is a man I want to thank. I want to show everyone how important he is. What should I do for this man?" asked the king.

Haman thought the king was talking about him. So Haman said, "Let him wear your robe. Let someone important lead him on your horse, calling, 'This is what the king does for the man he wants to honor!'"

"All right," said the king to Haman. "Then go and get the robe and the horse, and do just what you have said. Do all of those things for Mordecai."

Haman had to give Mordecai the king's robe and lead Mordecai around on the king's horse. Haman had to call out to everyone, "This is what the king does for the man he wants to honor!"

So the lowly man became great and the great man became lowly on the night when the king could not sleep.

Who Brings Out the Stars?

JOB 1–6; 38–40; 42

There was once a man named Job. He was a good man. He loved and obeyed God. He was a rich man, too. He had a big family and thousands of animals—sheep and camels and oxen and donkeys.

But robbers came and took away everything Job owned. Job had nothing left. And then he got sick.

Job was sad and tired. But he still said, "I praise God. He is wise and powerful."

Job's friends came to see him. "You must have done something wrong," they said. "Or else these bad things wouldn't have happened."

But Job said, "What have I done wrong?"

Then God talked to Job. "What makes you so wise?" God asked him. "Where were you when I made the earth, when the morning stars sang and the angels shouted their joy? Who told the sea, 'This is as far as you can go—your waves must stop here'?"

Job knew the answer: God did that.

"Have you ever gone to the places where the snow is stored?" asked God. "Or to the place where the east winds begin? Who makes the ice and the frost?"

Job knew the answer: God does that.

"Can you bring out the stars?" God asked. "Can you talk to the clouds and bring rain? Do you send the lightning? Do you bring food to the birds?"

Job knew the answer: No! God does that.

"The ostrich's wings flap with joy," said God. "But she lays her eggs on the ground and lets them get warm in the sand. I did not make her wise. But she can run faster than a horse. Do you make the horse strong? Have you put a flowing mane on his neck? Do you make him rear up and snort?"

Job knew the answer: No! God does that.

"Do you show the hawk how to fly?" asked God. "Do you tell the eagle to build her nest on the cliff and to sleep there at night?"

Job knew the answer: No! God does that.

"Look how I made the elephant," said God. "His trunk sways. He is strong. He lies among the lotus plants and the reeds in the marsh. You see, everything under heaven is mine."

Job said, "I know that you can do all things, Lord. My ears had heard of you. But now I know you."

Then God blessed Job. God made Job healthy again. And God made him rich again. God gave Job twice as much as he had before!

All of Job's friends came to his house for dinner. Each friend brought a piece of silver and a gold ring for Job. And Job became the greatest man in the East. But he never stopped loving and obeying God.

Looking at the Stars

PSALM 8

When night comes to the countryside, over the hills and in the valleys, the sheep settle down to go to sleep. But the shepherds don't go home. They stay in the fields and watch their sheep to make sure the sheep are safe.

When the shepherds are tired, they lie down outside. Sometimes the moon is big and full. Then the night is bright all around. Sometimes clouds cover the sky or the moon is a tiny sliver. Then the night is dark all around. Sometimes the night sky is clear and full of stars. Then the shepherds can look up at the quiet, deep, starry sky.

David was a shepherd boy. He spent many nights outside. When he looked at the stars, he thought about God. And he wrote songs about God.

One time David wrote:

"O Lord, your name is the greatest in the world.

Your power shines from above the skies.

You planned for children
to sing of your wonderful name,

so that anyone who does not love you
will have to be quiet.

When I look at the skies
that you made with your own hands,
and when I see the moon and stars
that you put in their special places,
people don't seem very important at all.

And I wonder why you care about people.

But you made us almost as important as you.

You let us be in charge
of what you have made:
the sheep and cows and animals in the fields,
the birds and fish and sea animals.

Oh, Lord, your name is the greatest
in the world!"

When night comes and you look at the starry sky, what do you think
about God?

Vegetables and Water, Please

DANIEL 1

The big stone walls of the city of Babylon towered over a wide river. The city was in a country by the same name—Babylon. The mighty army of Babylon marched into the city through the tall arched gate covered with blue tiles. With the army came Daniel and his three friends and other young men. They were God's people, who were being moved to this new city far away from home. They were going to work for the famous king of Babylon.

Daniel and his friends were strong. They were healthy. They were good-looking. They were smart, too. That's why they had been chosen to come to Babylon. The king of Babylon wanted all these young men to learn all about his country. Then the king would choose the best young men to serve him in the beautiful royal palace.

While the young men were learning about Babylon, the king treated them as special guests. Every day he sent them the very best food that his own cooks had made: savory meats, rich creamy sauces, thick chewy breads, sweet treats, and wines.

But Daniel and his friends knew that these were not the kinds of foods that God wanted them to eat. So they asked the king's chief servant to bring them vegetables and water instead.

Now the chief servant liked Daniel and his friends. But he was afraid of the king. "If you don't eat the king's food, you won't be strong," he said. "Your faces will turn pale. When the king sees how weak you are and how strong the other young men are, he will be angry with me."

But Daniel said, "Let us try vegetables and water for just ten days. Then see how we look."

So the chief servant let them eat only vegetables and drink only water for ten days. At the end of the ten days, he was surprised. Daniel and his friends looked stronger and healthier than all the other young men. So he brought them vegetables and water for all their meals.

God made Daniel and his three friends very wise. They easily learned language and science. They knew all the writings in the best books of the kingdom. And when their three years of learning were over, the king decided that Daniel and his three friends were the wisest of all the young men. So he chose them to work with him at his beautiful royal palace.

No Roars Tonight!

DANIEL 6

The leaders sneaked around, watching Daniel. They followed him because the king was going to make Daniel their boss. And they were jealous. So they were watching for Daniel to do something wrong. But he didn't. Daniel was good and wise, and he did what was right.

"We'll have to trap Daniel!" said the leaders. So they whispered among themselves. And they came up with a sneaky plan. They went to the king and said, "We think you should make a law that says everyone has to pray to you. If people don't do it, they'll be thrown into a cave full of lions."

So the king made that law. He wrote it down in the law books. That meant the law could not be changed.

Daniel heard about the new law. But he went right upstairs to his open window. He got down on his knees and prayed to God— just like he always did.

The leaders were watching. Their trap had worked. So they went back to the king. "Daniel is not obeying you," they said. "He prays to his God three times every day."

This news made the king very upset. He liked Daniel. He tried everything he could think of to keep from throwing Daniel into the cave of hungry lions.

But when the sun went down that evening, the leaders came back to the king. "You can't change your law," they said.

The king knew they were right. So Daniel was thrown to the lions. The king called to him, "Daniel, I hope your God will save you!" Then a huge rock was rolled across the opening of the cave.

The king went back to his palace. But he couldn't sleep that night. He didn't even feel like eating or doing anything for fun.

As soon as the sun started coming up, the king rushed to the lions' cave. He called, "Daniel, did your God save you?"

"Yes, my king," called Daniel. "God sent his angel to be with me. The angel made the lions close their mouths. They didn't hurt me at all!"

The king was so excited! He ordered men to help Daniel out of the cave. Then he wrote a new law to all his people. This law said, "People everywhere in my kingdom must respect Daniel's God. Daniel's God lives forever. He keeps his people safe. And his kingdom will never end."

A Ride inside a Fish

JONAH 1–3

Big ships and little boats gently bobbed up and down, tied to the docks at the seaport. Oxen pulled loaded carts along the shore, clattering over the rocky pathways. Bundles and boxes and bags sat in piles. Sailors pulled on the rope riggings and shouted directions to each other. People scurried here and there, getting ready to sail. And one man hurried among them on his way to buy a ticket.

"A ticket to Tarshish, please," said Jonah. He paid his money and took his ticket. Soon he was walking up the ramp to get on board the ship. *Maybe this will be a good place to hide,* he thought.

Jonah was running away. God had told Jonah to go to the big city of Nineveh and tell the people that they were in trouble for doing wrong things. But Jonah didn't want to. So he went the other way. Now he was going to sail on a ship to get away from God.

It wasn't long until the ramp to the dock was pulled away with a scrape and a bump. The ropes to the dock were untied. Sailors raised the wide cloth sail. It flapped and filled with the ocean air, and the ship sailed out of the harbor.

Jonah took a deep breath. At last they were on their way. He climbed down into the ship, leaned back on his pack, and went to sleep.

But a strong, gusty windstorm blew in, churning up the sea. Waves dashed against the ship, driving it up and down. And there was Jonah, sound asleep.

"Wake up and pray to your God!" shouted the captain. "Maybe he will help us! We don't know why this terrible storm has hit us!"

But Jonah knew why. "It's my fault," he said. "I was trying to run away from God."

"Oh no!" cried the sailors. "What should we do?"

"Throw me out of the ship," said Jonah.

The sailors didn't want to throw Jonah out. But the storm got worse and worse. At last they threw Jonah overboard into the wild crashing waves.

Right away the storm stopped. Then the sailors believed in God. And they sailed on.

But Jonah sank down, down into the sea. Suddenly—*gulp!*—
a big fish swallowed Jonah. He gasped and sputtered. "You saved
me, oh, God," said Jonah. "I will keep my promises to you."

For three days and three nights, Jonah prayed in the fish's
soggy, sloppy belly. But at last the fish spit up Jonah on the beach.

"Get up," God told Jonah. "Go to the city of Nineveh. Tell
the people there that they are in trouble with me unless they
change."

Jonah knew that God was right. And this time, Jonah obeyed.

NEW TESTAMENT

Hay Bed

LUKE 2:1-20

Clatter, rattle, bump. Clip-clip, clip-clop. Step, step, shuffle, shuffle. Along the dirt road came the people—some with carts, some riding donkeys, some just walking.

Mary was riding a donkey. She had to. She was carrying a big load herself. A baby was growing inside her, and it was almost time for the baby to be born. Now, Mary carried a special secret in her heart: The baby was God's Son!

Joseph, who was Mary's husband, walked beside Mary. He knew the secret, too. But the other people around them didn't know. And there were more and more people on the road the closer they got to Bethlehem. They were all going back to be counted with the other people whose families had come from Bethlehem.

The streets of Bethlehem were full of people and carts and animals. Joseph pushed through the crowds, leading Mary's donkey. They found their way to the inn. Mary was tired. She was ready to rest for a while. But there wasn't any room at the inn. In fact, there wasn't any room at *any* house. There were so many people in Bethlehem that all the beds were already taken.

But Mary couldn't spend the night in the street! Joseph had to find a place for them. And he finally did. He found a stable. There were donkeys and cows in the stable, but there was room for Mary and Joseph, too.

What a surprise to come to Bethlehem and have to spend the night in a stable! Then Joseph and Mary had another surprise!

The baby came, red-faced and crying. But what a wonderful baby he was!

God himself wanted to tell the world that his Son had been born. So he sent angels during the night to the fields outside the town.

Sheep slept, like big white fluffy balls, snuggled in groups across the shadowy hills. All of a sudden, an angel appeared. The shepherds shook with fear.

"Don't be afraid," said the angel. "I have good news from God! Today in Bethlehem God's Son was born! If you want to go see the baby, you can find him in a manger of hay."

Suddenly, lots of angels appeared. They said, "Glory to God, and peace to men."

When the angels left, the shepherds said, "Wow! Let's go to Bethlehem. Let's see what the angels were talking about!"

They rushed to town and looked for the baby. And they found him right where the angel had said he would be—in a manger, a bed of hay. He was a tiny baby, but he was God's Son!

One Bright Star

MATTHEW 2:1-12

Night after night they watched the skies. They counted stars. They looked at the shapes the stars made: a bear, a lion, a fish. They noticed which stars were bright and which stars were dim. They saw how the stars changed from season to season. They were the Magi, the wise men from eastern lands.

One night as the Magi studied the stars, they saw a new star— a very bright star. "This is an important star," they said.

"It is a sign," they said.

"It means that a new baby king has been born. We have to go find him and worship him," they said. "This baby must be a very important king to have such a bright star!"

So the wise men packed gifts for the new baby king, and they began their long trip. They traveled over hills. They traveled across valleys. They went through dry, sandy deserts. They crossed rivers. And the star led them. Every night, there it was, showing the way.

At last the wise men came to the big city of Jerusalem. They stopped to ask if anyone knew where the baby king was. "We come from the east, where we first saw his star," they said. "We have come to worship him."

King Herod heard that the wise men were asking about a new baby king. So he called the leaders of his people together. "Do you know anything about a new king?" he asked.

"We know that long ago a man named Micah wrote about a king who would come from Bethlehem," said the leaders.

King Herod called for the wise men. "Go to Bethlehem," he said. "Find this new baby king. Then come and tell me where he is. I want to worship him, too."

So that night the wise men looked at the sky again. The star was still there. They followed it all the way to Bethlehem.

The star stopped right over the house where Mary and little Jesus were.

The wise men went in and bowed down. They worshiped Jesus. They opened up their packs of gifts: gold and sweet-smelling incense and myrrh. They left these gifts for little Jesus.

Then God told the wise men not to tell King Herod where Jesus was.

Because they were so wise, the Magi went home a different way. Over hills, across valleys, through deserts, and across rivers, they traveled home, studying the stars all the way.

Nothing Left to Drink

JOHN 2:1-11

Music was playing. People dressed in their fine clothes were dancing and laughing and singing. They had come to celebrate with the bride and groom at a wedding party.

Food filled the bowls and plates on the table: breads and meats and yummy sweet treats. The servants filled glasses with sparkling wine. People ate and drank and enjoyed the party.

Jesus and his mother enjoyed the party, too. They laughed and talked and celebrated with everyone else. But in a little while Jesus' mother called him to come into the next room with her. She looked worried. "Something terrible has happened," she said. "They have run out of wine!"

The party was not over yet. There was plenty of food left but nothing left to drink.

Jesus looked around. Six big, stone water jars stood next to the wall. They were used to hold fresh water for washing. "Fill these jars to the top with water," Jesus told the servants.

So the servants did what Jesus asked, sloshing the water into the big stone jars.

When the last drop of water had been poured into the jars, Jesus said, "Dip some of it out now, and take it to the man in charge of the party."

So a servant plopped a dipper down into one of the jars of water. When he lifted the dipper out, wine was dripping from it! The jar was full of wine. It was not water anymore!

The servants laughed. They could hardly believe it. They took the new wine to the man in charge.

The man in charge of the party sipped the wine, and his eyes brightened. He didn't know where this wine had come from. He called to the groom. "Most people serve the best wine first," he said. "But this is the best wine! And you have saved it until now!"

So there was plenty of food and plenty of wine. People ate and drank and danced and sang. And everyone enjoyed the party.

A Hole in the Roof

MARK 2:1-12; LUKE 5:17-26

Gently, gently four friends lifted the man who could not move. They were sad for him because when they walked to town, he could not walk with them. When they sat around the table to talk and eat, he could not sit with them. When they worked together in the field, he could not work with them. When they went fishing, he could not fish with them. They wanted him to be well again because he was their friend.

So when these friends heard that Jesus was in town, they gently, gently took hold of the corners of their friend's bed mat. They lifted him while he was lying down on his mat. Together they carried their friend down the road, past the worship house, past the marketplace, to the house where Jesus was staying.

But before they even got close to the house, their steps slowed down. They began to frown. They could hardly see the house where Jesus was staying. People were standing in a crowd around the door. Some were standing on tiptoe at the windows, listening from the outside. The house was so crowded! There was no room for four men carrying their friend on a mat.

"Now what will we do?" asked the first friend.

"There must be a way to get in," said the second friend.

"There are people at all the windows and people at all the doors," said the third friend.

"But there are no people on the roof," said the fourth friend. "Come on! I have an idea!"

Gently, gently the four friends carried the man on his mat up the

outside stairs onto the roof. *Scratch, scratch, tap, tap, dig, dig.* They began making a hole in the dried-clay roof.

At first the hole was small. Then it got bigger and bigger as the men lifted the clay tiles out of the way. When the hole looked big enough, they tied ropes around their friend's mat. Then gently, gently they let it down through the roof until their friend was lying on his mat right in front of Jesus.

The people standing around Jesus dusted crumbs of clay and roof dirt off of their clothes and out of their hair.

But Jesus smiled as he looked at the man on the mat. "You can get up and go home now," Jesus said. "And don't forget to take your mat with you."

The man jumped up, stretching his arms and legs. He grinned at Jesus, picked up his mat, and squeezed through the crowd of staring people until he popped out of the house into the sunshine.

There were his four friends waiting for him, praising God, and looking for something to do together!

The Man by the Pool
JOHN 5:1-15

Swish, swish, bubble, bubble. The water in the clear pool swirled around.

"Ooh!" murmured the people sitting under the covered porches around the pool. Some of them leaned forward and began shuffling, limping, and scooting toward the pool.

An old woman got to the pool first. She stuck her feet in. A girl helped the woman ease herself down into the water. "Aah!" said the old woman, closing her eyes and relaxing in the warm bubbly water.

The other people sat back down and waited for the water to bubble and swirl again. It was said that an angel stirred up the water. If someone who was sick could be the first to get into the swirling water, that person would be made well again.

A man lying at the side of the pool sighed. He had been sick for 38 years! He tried to be the first one in the water. But he had no one to help him get in. So someone else always got there first. The sick man sighed again and shook his head.

Just then Jesus walked by. He looked at the sick man. "Do you want to be well?" asked Jesus.

"Yes," said the man. "I have tried to get into the water, but somebody always gets there before I can get in."

"I see," said Jesus. "Then stand up, pick up your mat, and walk."

The man's eyes grew wide. He slowly bent his knees. He put his feet flat on the ground. He slowly stood up. His feet and legs felt

different. They felt new and strong. The man took one step and then another. He could walk!

The man rolled up his mat and tucked it under his arm. Then, left foot, right foot, left foot, right foot, he strolled across the walkway under the porches. He stepped out into the street, walked past the Sheep Gate, and headed down the road, straight and tall, thankful for his new, strong legs.

Spending the Night on a Mountain

MATTHEW 6:9-13; LUKE 6:12-16; LUKE 11:1-4

Up, up, up Jesus went, walking up the mountainside. Over grass and over rocks he climbed until he got to a special place where he could be alone.

He thought about God, his Father. He knew God was thinking about him. He knew God was with him. So he began to talk with God. He prayed. And he listened.

Late afternoon came. The sky was filled with a rosy glow, and the sun sank low. Shadows grew long. Still Jesus prayed. And he listened.

The clouds turned gold and pink and red as the sun set in the west. Still Jesus prayed. And he listened.

Stars began to twinkle here and there in the evening sky. Still Jesus prayed. And he listened.

The sky turned dark blue-purple and then black. The moon climbed higher in the sky. Still Jesus prayed and listened and prayed.

Nighttime passed by. Little by little, in the east, the sky began to get lighter. A line of rosy pink showed. And then yellow. And then the sun peeked up over the hills. Jesus had prayed all night long!

Jesus walked back down the mountain. Then he chose 12 men to be his very special friends. They went places with him, and they helped him.

One day Jesus' special friends asked him to teach them how to pray. So he did. Jesus said, "When you pray, here's what you can say.

Father in heaven,
your name is the most special of all.

You are the King,
so bring your kingdom to the whole earth.

Let things happen your way on earth
the way things happen in heaven.

Give us the food we need to eat each day.

Forgive us for what we do wrong.

Don't let us be tempted to do wrong.

Keep us away from bad things.

The kingdom is yours forever.

Power is yours forever.

Glory is yours forever.
Amen."

Ravens and Lilies

MATTHEW 6:25-34; 8:14-17; 10:29-31

Ravens flapped their wings and glided overhead. They landed nearby and pecked around. The grass swished in the breeze. The lilies nodded with their petals stretched out, open to the warm sun's rays. And a crowd of people sat around Jesus, listening.

"Don't worry about what you'll eat," said Jesus. "Just look at the birds. They don't plant seeds. They don't grow their own food. They don't have barns to store food in. God feeds them. And you are much more important than birds! So God will take care of you.

"Look at the lilies. They don't make their own clothes. But even King Solomon's clothes were no more beautiful than the lilies. You are much more important than lilies! If God takes care of lilies, he will take care of you, too. If you love and obey God, he will make sure you have everything you need."

Another time Jesus said, "Here's how important you are to God. Think about little sparrows. They are common birds. There are lots of them around. But God doesn't forget about any of them. So don't be afraid. To God, you are more important than many sparrows. If God watches over the sparrows, he will watch over you, too. God even knows how many hairs you have on your head!"

Jesus said that God loves you very much. Jesus said that you are important to God. Jesus said that God gives you good things.

One day when Jesus went to Peter's house, he saw that Peter's mother was sick. She had a high fever. She wasn't famous. She

wasn't rich. But God knew who she was. She was important to God. And Jesus made her well.

That evening, when the sun was going down, lots of sick people came to see Jesus: sick men, sick women, sick boys, and sick girls. They weren't famous, and they weren't rich. But God knew who each one was. Each one of them was important to God. Jesus touched every sick person, one by one. And all of them got well.

When those people went home that night, they went home feeling great! They were well! And as they lay down to sleep, they knew they were important to God. They knew God loved them.

Just Say the Word

LUKE 7:1-10

The captain used to smile when he thought about his servant. What a good servant he had! This servant was always ready to help. He did a good, careful job no matter what he had to do. He was cheerful, too. The captain loved his servant.

But today when the captain thought about his servant, he looked sad. He was worried because his servant was sick. For several days his servant had been in bed, tossing and turning, burning hot with fever. The captain had hoped his servant would be better by now. Instead, the man had gotten worse. Now the captain knew that if he didn't get help right away, his servant would die.

The captain had heard that Jesus was coming to town. So he called some leaders and asked them to find Jesus. "Ask Jesus to come and heal my servant," said the captain.

So the leaders looked for Jesus, and they found him. "Jesus," they said, "the captain has sent us. He is a good man. He loves God's people. He even built a worship house for us. But his servant is very sick. He will die if you don't heal him. Please come with us to the captain's house."

"All right," said Jesus. "I'll come."

So they walked down narrow streets and wide streets, past small houses and big houses and shops. But when they got close to the captain's house, a small group of men came up to them. These were some of the captain's friends.

"The captain has sent us," they said. "He knows that you are very important. He says to tell you not to go to the trouble of coming into his house. He says that if you will just say the word, right where you are, his servant will get well. The captain knows that just as the men in his army have to obey him, so this sickness has to obey you. So if you will say the word, his servant will be well."

Jesus turned around to the crowd of people that was following him. "I've never seen anyone who believes in me as much as this captain does," said Jesus.

Then the captain's friends knew that what the captain believed was really going to happen. And by the time the friends got back to the captain's house, his servant was completely well!

Asleep in a Storm

LUKE 8:22-25

Gray clouds skimmed across the sky above the lake. A breezy wind flapped Jesus' robe as he stood in the boat. He had been teaching as he always did. Lots of people had been listening to him teach.

But now Jesus was tired. The evening sky was dim and dusky. The lake water rippled and slapped the sides of the boat. "Let's go to the other side of the lake," said Jesus.

So Jesus' friends headed the boat toward the other side of the lake. They left the crowd of people behind them.

Jesus went to the back of the boat. There was a pillow back there. He lay down on the pillow and soon fell fast asleep. The boat rocked back and forth.

But the sky grew darker. The wind blew harder. The waves grew higher. The boat swayed in the waves. And still Jesus slept.

Night was coming. But now the wind came in great gusts. The waves leaped into the air and came crashing into the boat. And still Jesus slept.

Down dipped the boat. Up bobbed the boat. *Crash* came the waves. Down, up, *crash, splash!*

Jesus' friends tried to keep the boat sailing smoothly. But they couldn't. Down, up, *crash, splash!* Water was sloshing around in the boat now. And there was Jesus in the back of the boat, sleeping!

"Wake up, Jesus! Wake up!" called his friends. "We're going to drown!"

Jesus got up. But he didn't help his friends bail the water out ofthe boat. He didn't help them try to steer it. He didn't tell them what to do. Instead, he talked to the wind. He talked to the waves. "Hush!" he said. "You be still!"

The wind slowed down to a whisper. The waves settled down and went back to a peaceful ripple. Everything was calm.

"Your faith is very small," Jesus said to his friends.

"Wow!" said his friends. "Even the winds and waves obey Jesus!"

And they sailed calmly on to the other side of the lake on that beautiful, peaceful night.

A Small Woman
in a Big Crowd

MARK 5:21, 25-34; LUKE 8:43-48

A big crowd of people stood at the side of the lake. They put their hands over their eyes to shade them from the glare of the sun so they could see. They peered into each boat that passed. Strong men rowed some of the boats. Puffy sails, filled by the wind, pulled other boats along. Which boat would Jesus be riding in?

"Here he comes!" called someone. "He's in that boat over there!"

The people moved over to the place where Jesus' boat would be landing. It was so exciting to have Jesus come!

As Jesus walked into town, people joined him, shuffling and strolling, squeezing closer here and there, talking and clamoring to say something to Jesus.

One small thin woman on the edge of the crowd wanted very much to be right in the middle. She had been sick for 12 years. She had spent all her money paying doctors. But none of them could help her. She hoped now that Jesus would make her well.

But how could she even ask Jesus to help, with all these people around? Jesus would never hear her if she called out to him. He would never see her among all the people. *If I could just touch Jesus' robe, I'd be well,* she thought.

So this small thin woman began squeezing in between other people, pushing her way toward Jesus. She got bumped and jostled. Her toes got stepped on. People talked loudly—right in her ears! But she kept inching closer to Jesus. Little by little she scooted in. And then, there he was, right in front of her! Her heart was beating so fast she could hear it. She reached out. Almost, almost—there! She touched the edge of Jesus' robe.

Right away, the woman could feel it. She was stronger. No more hurting. She knew. She had been healed!

But suddenly Jesus stood still. He turned around. "Who touched my robe?" he asked.

The woman held her breath. How did Jesus know? She was already small, but she wished she could shrink and become even smaller and run away.

One of Jesus' friends said, "Jesus, how can you ask who touched you? Everyone in this big crowd is pushing against you."

But Jesus kept looking around for a face. "Someone touched me for a reason," Jesus said. "I felt healing power go out from me."

The small thin woman was shaking, but she knew that she had to tell him. She bowed down on her knees. "I touched you," she said. "I was sick, and I wanted to be well again. I touched your robe, and I was healed."

Then Jesus smiled and softly said, "Daughter."

The small thin woman looked up into Jesus' eyes. She smiled shyly.

"Go in peace," said Jesus. "You are well because you believe in me."

Supper for Everyone

JOHN 6:1-13

Green grass, puffy white clouds, a blue sky, lots of sunshine—it had been a beautiful day to sit outside. And lots of people had come—more than five thousand people! Tall and short, stout and thin, young and old, they had come to see Jesus. Sick people came to see Jesus too. He made them well.

All the people stayed to listen to what Jesus had to say. And he told them about God.

But now the shadows were growing longer as the sun moved across the sky. People were starting to get hungry. Jesus turned to his friend Philip. "Where can we buy some food for these people?" Jesus asked.

"We don't have enough money to buy food for all these people!" said Philip. "Why, we could work for eight months, and we still would not have enough money to buy even one little bite for everyone!"

Then Andrew said, "Look! Here's someone who was smart!" He pointed to a little boy who had brought his supper with him.

The little boy held out his small bundle of food to Jesus.

"Just five small rolls and two small fish!" said Andrew. "That's not enough food for all these people!"

But Jesus took the five small rolls. "Tell everyone to sit down," said Jesus.

So Jesus' friends started passing the message around: "Sit down on the grass."

"Sit down," said the short people to the tall people.

"Sit down," said the stout people to the thin people.

"Sit down," said the old people to the young people. "Jesus says to sit down!"

All the people sat on the soft, soft grass.

Jesus thanked God for the bread. He broke it into pieces and passed it around.

Then Jesus' friends helped until everyone—short and tall, stout and thin, young and old—had bread to eat!

Jesus looked at the little boy again.

The boy held out his two small fish.

Jesus smiled and took the fish. He thanked God for them. Then he handed fish to the people. Short and tall, stout and thin, young and old—everyone soon had fish to eat!

Even the little boy got some of his own bread and fish to eat!

All of the people ate until they were full. And when they were finished, Jesus said, "Let's pick up the leftovers now so we don't waste any food."

Jesus' friends got some baskets and began cleaning up. *Plop, plop, plop.* Leftover bread and leftover fish went into the baskets. *Plop, plop, plop!* Twelve baskets full!

Soon people began to walk home. Short people, tall people, stout people, thin people, young people, old people—these were happy people with full tummies. And it was all because one little boy shared!

Stopping to Help

LUKE 10:30-35

A Story That Jesus Told

The road was long and the trip was lonely. High rocky hills stood along the way. Twisted, scraggly trees and bushes lined small streams.

It was dangerous to travel this road alone. But down the road trudged a lone traveler with a full pack on his back.

The traveler kept a close watch for any dangers that might lie ahead. Even so, he couldn't see behind all the rocks or under all the bushes. All at once, a gang of robbers jumped out at him. They took his pack. They hit him hard. He fell down hurt on the dusty, rocky road. The robbers took everything he had, and they ran away through the bushes and over the rocky hills.

The man was hurting so badly, he couldn't get up. He needed help.

After a while, the traveler heard footsteps. They came closer and

closer. The traveler groaned. He hoped that whoever was coming would hear him and stop to help. He opened his eyes a little to see who it was. Good news! This was a man of God, a priest from the temple, dressed in his rich clothes. Surely he would stop and help.

Closer and closer the priest came. But then he crossed to the other side of the road! He didn't even look twice at the hurting traveler.

It wasn't long before the hurt man heard more footsteps. He groaned again, hoping this person would help. He opened his eyes and looked. Good news! This was not a priest, but it was a man who worked at the temple. This man would surely help.

But as the footsteps got closer and closer, they also got faster and faster. This man crossed over to the other side of the road, too.

The hurt traveler closed his eyes again. In a little while he heard a *clip, cloppin'* of donkey hooves against the hard dirt road. The traveler opened his eyes a little bit. Bad news. It was a man from a different country riding toward him on a donkey. And the people from the hurt man's country were not even friendly to people from the stranger's country. So he certainly wouldn't want to stop. The hurt man groaned.

But the donkey's steps slowed down. They stopped. The next thing the hurt man knew, this stranger was giving him a drink, cleaning off his hurt places, and helping him up onto the donkey.

Slowly they made their way down the road to an inn where travelers could stay. As the sun went down that night, the hurt traveler found himself in a soft bed, sipping warm broth, resting and feeling better.

The traveler knew then that it doesn't matter how people look or where they are from. Real friends are those people who help.

So Much to Do

LUKE 10:38-42

There was so much to do! So much to do! Martha looked around. She hardly knew where to start. Jesus was in town. Martha had told Jesus that he could stay at her house with her and her sister, Mary, and their brother, Lazarus. And Jesus had said yes!

Now there was so much to do to get ready. Floors to sweep. Dinner to cook. Fresh clean covers for the bed mats.

Mary and Martha both worked. *Sweep, sweep, sweep* went the broom. *Clink, clink, clink* went the dishes as they were set out. *Slosh, slosh, slosh* went the water that Mary brought from the well. *Sweep, sweep, sweep* and *clink, clink, clink* and *slosh, slosh, slosh*. And *knock, knock, knock*.

Knock, knock, knock?

Someone's at the door! Hurry! Answer the door!

"I'll get it!"

"I'll get it!"

Mary and Martha answered the door. There was Jesus. "Come in! Come in! Welcome to our house!"

But Martha had not finished working. She ran back to work. *Stir, stir, stir. Mix, mix, mix.* Oops! Wipe up the spill! *Where's Mary?* thought Martha. *She should be helping me.*

Martha went to find Mary. And there Mary sat—at Jesus' feet! She was just listening! "Jesus!" said Martha. "Mary has left me to do all the work by myself! Tell her to come and help me."

Jesus smiled at Martha. He said, "Martha, Martha, you are so worried about every little thing! Mary has chosen to do the only thing that's really important. I won't keep her from being with me!"

Martha thought about it. There would always be work to do. Right now, the important thing was just to spend time with Jesus.

Sheep and Shepherd

A Story That Jesus Told

LUKE 15:3-7; JOHN 10:3-5, 14

One hundred sheep maaing and baaing. One hundred sheep clipping and clopping over the rocks to find sprigs of grass. One hundred sheep nibbling and chewing. One hundred sheep sleeping and snoozing in the cool shade of the trees.

The good shepherd watches and keeps all of the sheep together. He finds cool water for them to drink. He finds fresh patches of sweet, tender grass for them to eat. He calls them and leads them, his one hundred sheep. And once in a while he counts them to make sure they are all with him.

But one day he counts and, uh-oh. Where is that funny little sheep? That funny, wandering, headstrong sheep? Has he wandered away?

He is in danger all by himself. He needs the good shepherd to watch over him. So the good shepherd looks for his wandering sheep—over the hills, behind the bushes, by the river, below the cliffs.

The good shepherd listens. He hears the bubbling brook and the cawing ravens. He hears buzzing bugs and chattering squirrels. And then he hears the maaing and baaing of one little sheep. One funny, wandering, headstrong sheep.

And the shepherd walks toward the baaing sound to find his wandering sheep.

The shepherd picks up the wandering sheep. He hugs that oily, soft, plump, woolly sheep. And he carries his sheep all the way home, back to the maaing, baaing flock, sleeping and snoozing in the starry night.

You are Jesus' little sheep.

"I am the good shepherd," said Jesus. "I know my sheep, and my sheep know me. I call each of my sheep by name. I lead them, and they go with me. I take care of my sheep. I never leave them. They are safe with me."

The Man Who Remembered

LUKE 17:11-19

Ten men—ten sad men. They lived together away from other people. They cooked together and ate together. They talked together and walked together. They could look at the city in the distance where their homes were. But they could not go there.

They could watch carts and donkeys and people moving down the road to the city. But they could not get close. They could not touch anyone. They had to stay away because they had very bad sores on their skin. If they got too close to other people, the other people might get the sores, too.

Only the priest let people with that sickness get near him. He could look at their skin and tell them if they were getting well. If they were well, they could go back home to their families in the city. If they were not well, the priest would send them away again.

Now these ten men had heard about Jesus. They had heard that Jesus made people well. If they could just get to Jesus, maybe he could make them well, too. But they knew they could not go into any town to look for Jesus because they all had bad sores on their skin.

One day the ten men heard that Jesus was coming to a town near them. They hurried to get as close to the town as they could. Then they waited and watched for Jesus to come down the road.

Clop, clop, clop, rattledy, rattle. They looked. Was it Jesus? No. It was only some oxen pulling a cart of grain.

Maa, maa, scuffle scuffle. Was Jesus coming? No. It was only a herd of goats being prodded along by a little boy and his father.

Then one man saw something in the distance. "Look! What's that?" he said.

The ten men watched. They saw a small group of people coming down the road. Was Jesus one of them? Which one?

"Jesus!" called the ten men.

The people on the road looked at the men and slowed down. One man stepped forward. It was Jesus.

"Jesus, be kind to us," called the ten sick men.

Jesus smiled and pointed toward the town. "Go and let the priest take a look at you," he said.

The ten sick men looked at each other for a minute. This was interesting. Jesus had told them to go to the priest. "All right," they said. "We'll go." They started walking toward the town.

One man looked down at his hand. "Hey! I'm well!" he said. He began walking faster.

The others began to look at their skin. They began to look at each

other's skin. "I'm well! You're well! We're all well!" They began running to the town.

Then one of the men stopped. He looked back down the road. Where was Jesus? Yes! He was still coming toward town with his friends.

The man ran back toward Jesus. He was so glad to be well! He shouted, "I'm well again!"

When he reached Jesus, the man bowed down to the ground right at Jesus' feet. "Thank you, Jesus," he said.

"Didn't I make ten men well?" asked Jesus. "Where are the other nine?" Then Jesus told the man, "Stand up. You are well now because you believe in me."

The man did stand up. And he went on his way, praising God.

In Jesus' Arms

MARK 10:13-16

There were giggles and whispers as the boys and girls came down the path. Some of them ran ahead. Some of them lagged behind. Some of them held hands. Some of them were just babies, so their mommies and daddies carried them.

As they got closer, they slowed down and looked. They could see Jesus talking with some men.

They walked closer. Their feet made shuffling sounds on the dirt. Some of the men looked up and frowned. Some of the men stepped closer to the mommies and daddies.

"We want Jesus to touch our children and pray for them," said the mommies and daddies.

But the men said, "You can't bring these children to see Jesus. He is busy right now."

Jesus looked up and saw the children. He smiled and reached out to them. "Let the children come," he said. "Don't stop them. God's kingdom belongs to children."

So the children came. They looked up at Jesus' face. He was smiling. They could tell that he was a lot of fun. Jesus picked up each child. And all of them hugged him as he prayed for them. In his arms they felt warm and safe.

The children went home skipping and giggling and whispering. They had seen Jesus!

Eyes to See

MARK 10:46-52

Every day blind Bartimaeus sat by the side of the road. When it was springtime, he could tell by the feel of the warm breeze and the scent of the wildflowers. When it was autumn, he could tell by the crisp chill of the air and by the smell of herbs, onions, wheat, and melons that farmers brought to market in their creaking carts.

Oh yes, Bartimaeus knew everything that happened on that road. He heard the sharp voices of the arguing leaders. He heard laughing, squealing children chasing in and out around their parents. He heard fussy babies and their mothers shushing them. He heard shuffling, tired old travelers leading clopping donkeys. He heard flocks of baaing sheep called into line by young shepherd boys. He heard young girls giggling and whispering, carrying empty jars on the way to the well.

Bartimaeus longed to see what he heard. But all he could do was hold out his hand and beg, "Be kind to me. I need money, please."

Then one breezy day Bartimaeus heard whispering, laughing, and excited voices. He pulled his cloak around him as he listened. And he smiled because he understood. Jesus was coming down the road!

Bartimaeus's heart began to beat faster. He had heard about Jesus. Yes, Jesus could heal people. Even blind people.

Bartimaeus listened until he knew Jesus must be near. Then he called, "Jesus! Jesus! Be kind to me!"

"Hush!" said the people. "Stop making all that noise. Jesus doesn't want to be bothered by a blind beggar."

Do they think I'm going to ask Jesus for money? thought Bartimaeus. "Jesus," he called even louder. "Jesus, be kind to me!"

The crowd got quiet.

"Jesus is calling for you," someone told him.

Bartimaeus's heart beat faster. He stood up and threw down his cloak. He felt his way past rough coats and silky robes, past big, rough hands and small, soft fingers.

Then Bartimaeus stood still. He knew he was there, holding his hand out in front of Jesus.

"What do you want?" asked Jesus.

"I want to see," said Bartimaeus. "I want to see!"

"All right," said Jesus. His voice was smiling. "You are well because you believe in me," said Jesus.

Bartimaeus blinked once, then twice. Was that Jesus he saw? Yes! It was Jesus! Bartimaeus turned around and around, wide-eyed. He could see it all: the faces—young and old, the trees, the road, the city, and Jesus. Yes! He could see Jesus.

As Jesus turned and walked on down the road, Bartimaeus was right behind, part of that big, noisy, laughing, talking crowd, following Jesus.

Where Will Jesus Stay?

LUKE 19:1-10

People rushed here and there, bustling around the city. Men combed their mustaches. Children combed their hair.

"Will Jesus stay at our house?" asked a boy.

"Maybe," said his mother. "If he knows that you've been good."

A leader of the town looked down his nose. "I think he'll stay at my house," said the man. "After all, I'm an important person in town."

People began to gather along the main street to watch for Jesus. Soon there was a crowd. They waved and laughed and chattered excitedly.

Then, from a shuttered window, a short, plump man peeked out. "What's all this noise about?" he asked.

But no one stopped to answer. It wasn't that the people didn't hear. It wasn't that they were in too much of a hurry. They didn't answer because they didn't like the man who asked the question. He was a rich tax collector named Zacchaeus. And everyone agreed that he collected too much tax. He seemed to get richer, while they got poorer.

Again Zacchaeus called out, "What's going on?"

Finally someone answered, "Jesus is coming to town!"

"Oh my!" exclaimed Zacchaeus. "I've heard about this man named Jesus! I wonder where he'll stay."

Zacchaeus joined the people crowding into the street. But he couldn't see. He was too short. So he tried to move around the people. But he saw only backs and belts. He stooped to look under.

But he just saw dust and feet. He jumped to see over. But he just saw heads and shoulders.

Zacchaeus sighed, "No room for me."

But then Zacchaeus had an idea. He looked up and around. Then he saw it—the perfect tree, wide and tall.

Zacchaeus ran to the tree. He climbed it very carefully. Higher

113

than the dust and feet. Higher than the belts and backs. Higher than the shoulders and heads. He was higher than them all.

"Here he comes!" someone shouted.

Zacchaeus looked down the road. It was true. Jesus was coming. Zacchaeus wished that he could hear what Jesus was saying. But at least he could see. In fact, he could see Jesus clearer and clearer because with every step, Jesus got closer and closer to his tree!

Wow! thought Zacchaeus. *I get to see Jesus pass by very close to me!*

But Zacchaeus was wrong. Jesus did not pass by. Jesus stopped.

"Where are you going to stay?" asked a town leader.

Jesus looked up. Zacchaeus blinked in amazement. Jesus was looking right at him.

Jesus smiled and pointed to Zacchaeus. "I'm going to stay with Zacchaeus," said Jesus. "Come on down, Zacchaeus, and show me where you live."

Zacchaeus came right down. His heart was beating fast! Jesus was going to stay at his house!

"At Zacchaeus's house?!" said the people. "Don't you know Zacchaeus does bad things? He is a sinner."

"I know," said Jesus. "But that's why I came. I came to find and help sinners."

"I know I have been a sinner," Zacchaeus said. "But now I want to do what's right. Any money I've taken I will gladly repay. I'll give back four times what I took. And I'll give away half of my things to poor people."

"This is a great day!" said Jesus. "My friend, you once were lost. But look! Now you have been saved!"

That night Zacchaeus grinned as he pulled his covers up under his chin. Jesus was asleep in the next room!

Zacchaeus thought about all that had happened that day. And as he blew out his candle, he knew he had a very special friend.

Sweet Perfume

JOHN 12:1-8

It was the end of the day. The sun was going down on a little town called Bethany. Yummy food smells drifted from one of the houses. Sounds of talking and laughing came from the house.

Someone was having a special dinner party. Jesus was the guest.

Jesus' friend Lazarus was there, too, with his sisters, Mary and Martha. Lazarus sat at the table with Jesus. Martha brought the food in. Mmmm! It smelled so good. And everyone was hungry.

But where was Mary? She wasn't sitting at the table. She wasn't helping Martha bring the food in. Mary had planned a surprise. She was in the other room getting it ready.

Her surprise was in a jar. Mary opened the jar and sniffed. Oh! It smelled like flowers. It was pure perfume. And it cost a lot of money.

Mary closed the jar and took it into the room where Jesus and his friends were eating and talking and laughing. Mary walked over to Jesus and kneeled by his feet. She opened the jar and poured the perfume on his feet. Then she dried his feet with her long hair.

The perfume smelled beautiful! The sweet smell filled the house!

Judas, one of Jesus' friends, said, "Look at all the perfume Mary wasted! She could have sold it and made some money. Then she could have given the money to help poor people."

But Judas wasn't interested in helping poor people. He was the one who kept the money bag for Jesus. Sometimes he stole some money. He wished he had the money from that perfume in his bag.

Jesus said, "Leave Mary alone! She has done something special."

It was true. Mary had done something very special. It was her way of saying, "I love you, Lord Jesus. You are my Lord and my King."

Down the Road on a Donkey

MATTHEW 21:1-11; LUKE 19:28-40

"Hee-haw," said the little donkey. "Hee-haw, hee-haw, hee-haw."

One of Jesus' friends patted the little gray-brown donkey. The other friend went to the post near the door where the donkey was tied. No one had ever ridden this little donkey before. Jesus' friend untied the donkey and led her down the dirt road. *Clip-clop, clippety-clop.*

Now, people had heard that Jesus was coming their way. Many of them spread their coats on the road so the donkey could walk on the soft coats. *Pat-a-da, pat-a-da, pat-a-da, pat.*

Other people had cut branches from trees in the fields. They ran ahead of the little donkey. They tossed the branches on the road for the donkey to walk on. *Crunchety-swash, crunchety-swash.*

The people smiled and laughed and called out, "Hosanna! Hosanna! Blessed is the one who comes in God's name. Hosanna in the highest!" They were treating Jesus like a king.

Clippety-clop, clippety-clop. Pat-a-da, pat-a-da, pat-a-da, pat. Crunchety-swash, crunchety-swash. "Hosanna! Hosanna! Hosanna in the highest!"

Some of the city leaders saw Jesus coming on the donkey. They heard the excited crowd shouting. "Tell the people to be quiet!" the leaders said to Jesus.

But Jesus just shook his head. "If the people were quiet right now, the rocks would shout!" he said. And on he went to the big city, riding on the little donkey that no one had ever ridden before.

Clippety-clop, clippety-clop. Pat-a-da, pat-a-da, pat-a-da, pat. Crunchety-swash, crunchety-swash. "Hosanna! Hosanna! Blessed is the one who comes in God's name! Hosanna in the highest!"

The Day
the Children Shouted

MATTHEW 21:12-17

The temple was a big building. It was made of cream-colored stones. Parts of the temple were covered with gold. When the sun shone on the gold, the temple glowed so brightly that people could hardly look at it. It was a beautiful place.

The temple was also a place to worship and pray. But some men had set up tables and benches outside in the temple yard. They brought doves and sheep and cows there to sell. Other men set up banks at their tables. They exchanged the money that people brought from different places for money they could use at the temple. The doves fluttered and cooed. The sheep baaed. The cows mooed. The money clinked and jingled and jangled. And all this noise was right in the temple yard, near the place where people had come to pray.

That made Jesus angry. He said, "Get these animals out of here! Take your bank somewhere else. This house is supposed to be a place to pray! But you have turned it into a shopping mall! And you're robbing the people, taking more money from them than belongs to you."

Now, while Jesus was at the temple, people who couldn't see came to him. So Jesus made them well. People who couldn't walk were brought to Jesus. So Jesus made them well.

The children who were watching and listening to Jesus got

excited! Jesus was doing such wonderful things! The children began shouting, "Hosanna! Hosanna! Hosanna!"

There were some teachers nearby who worked at the temple. And there were priests, too. These teachers and priests heard the children shouting. They also saw Jesus healing people. But they didn't think all of this was so wonderful.

The teachers and priests went to Jesus. "Do you hear what these children are saying?" they asked.

"Yes," said Jesus. "Do you remember what King David wrote about children long ago? David wrote: 'Lord, you want children to praise you.'"

Then Jesus left the temple. He went to spend the night in the town where his friends Mary and Martha lived.

Washing Feet

MATTHEW 26:26-29; JOHN 13:1-17

Lamps were glowing, lighting the big room upstairs. Savory smells of supper drifted through the air—herbs and bread and meat and sauce and wine. This was a feast time and a time for remembering God.

Sitting around the big wooden table were Jesus and his 12 good friends. Jesus looked at his friends. He knew it was almost time for him to go back to heaven to be with God, his Father.

Jesus got up from the table. While his friends talked and ate, Jesus took off his outer robe and laid it aside. He went to a table at the side of the room. He picked up a long towel, and he wrapped it around his waist. Then he picked up a jar of water and poured it into a big bowl. The water softly splashed into the bowl.

Light from the lamps made sparkling reflections in the clear, sloshing water as Jesus carried it across the room. He set the bowl on the floor by the table and began washing Judas's feet just like a servant would do. Then he dried Judas's feet with the towel and moved to Philip.

One by one, Jesus washed each of his friends' dusty, tired feet: Judas, Philip, Bartholomew, Simon, Matthew, James A., Thaddaeus, Thomas, Andrew, James Z., John. And then it was Peter's turn.

But Peter pulled his feet away. "Why should you wash my feet?" asked Peter. "That's a job for a servant. I can never let you wash my feet."

"That means you don't want to be a part of what I'm doing," said Jesus.

"Oh!" said Peter. "Then wash my feet. Wash my hands and my head, too!"

Jesus washed Peter's feet. Then he put the bowl of water away. He put his robe back on and sat down with his friends.

"Do you know what I just did?" asked Jesus. "I am your Lord and Teacher. But I served you by washing your feet. You should learn from what I did and serve others."

Jesus picked up some flat, brown bread. He thanked God for it and then broke it into pieces. He passed it around to his friends. "Eat this to remember me," he said.

Then Jesus poured wine into a cup. "Drink this to remember me," he said. "I am going away for a little while. But I'll be back. And someday I'll take you with me so that you can live with me forever!"

Sadness and Joy

MATTHEW 28:1-8; MARK 14:26, 32-50

It was dark. Jesus and his friends took oil lamps with them. Down the stairs they walked, then outside into the cool night air. As they walked down the street, people passed them here and there. But lots of people were already indoors for the night. The warm lights of the houses shone through windows, making squares and rectangles of light on the dark streets.

Jesus and his friends followed the streets to the city gate. Then they walked out of the city under the starry sky. Down the path through the little valley they went, then up a hill to the garden where they liked to go.

Jesus and his friends were all very tired now, so they sat down to rest. Jesus' friends could tell that something was wrong because Jesus was very sad. He went off through the olive trees and kneeled down to pray. But his friends kept falling asleep. Three times Jesus came back to them. He wanted his friends to pray too.

When Jesus came back the third time, he said to his friends, "It is time." Suddenly they heard voices. They saw torchlights coming closer and closer. Jesus' friends jumped up and watched.

The men with torches were guards who had come to take Jesus away. The leaders of God's people did not like Jesus. They were afraid all the people would follow Jesus instead of following them. So they had Jesus taken away. These selfish, angry leaders wanted Jesus to die.

But Jesus knew this was going to happen. God knew this was going to happen. Being put on a cross to die was the punishment that

Jesus took for our sins. Jesus came to take the blame for all the wrong things we've done. He died on the cross.

At first Jesus' friends could hardly believe it. Jesus had never done anything wrong. But little by little Jesus' friends started to understand.

Early the next Sunday morning some of the women who knew Jesus walked to the cave tomb. That's where Jesus' body had been laid after he died. These women were sad, and they were worried. A big stone had been rolled over the opening to the cave tomb. And soldiers were guarding the tomb. The women wanted to put sweet-smelling spices in the tomb with Jesus' body. But they didn't know how they would move the big stone. And they didn't know what the guards would say.

Suddenly the ground began to rumble and shake. Then bright as lightning, an angel with white, shining clothes came and rolled the stone away. Then the angel sat on the stone.

The guards were so scared that they fainted. And the women could hardly believe their eyes.

But the angel told them, "Don't be afraid. I know you're looking for Jesus. But he's not here. Hurry and tell all his friends that Jesus is alive!"

The women hurried back down the path. They were very happy now because they knew it was true—Jesus was alive!

Hidden by the Clouds
MATTHEW 28:18-20; LUKE 24:50-53; ACTS 1:9-12

Big clouds floated across the sky. Birds dived through the air, singing their cheery songs. Jesus and his friends walked slowly down the road. It was good to be together again. Jesus had been teaching his friends more and more about God and his ways. And now that Jesus had come back to life after dying, his friends were beginning to understand.

Jesus' friends understood that he was a heavenly king who had come so that people would not have to live apart from God. Jesus had taken the blame and the punishment. Now everyone who believed and let Jesus be their Lord could be one of God's children. It was just as if they had never sinned. Jesus' goodness was now their goodness! This was good news.

Jesus led his friends up Olive Mountain. He said to them, "I want you to tell everybody about me. Tell people in this land. Tell people in countries near and far. Tell them the good news that you have learned. And remember this: I will always be with you, to the very end."

Then Jesus lifted up his hands toward the sky. And he went up and up, higher and higher. He was soon so high that the clouds hid him.

Jesus' friends couldn't see him anymore. But they kept looking, squinting their eyes at the sky. They were amazed at what had happened!

Suddenly, two men dressed in white stood beside them. "What are you looking at?" asked the two men. "Jesus has gone to heaven. Someday he will come back in just the same way."

Jesus' friends looked at each other in amazement. Then they began walking back toward town, laughing and talking and praising God.

Leaping for Joy

ACTS 3:1-11

It was the middle of the afternoon. Little boys and girls were taking a nap. Even some old men sat in the shade and dozed. People came down the street from the marketplace carrying bundles or baskets.

Peter and John talked as they walked down the street toward the big temple. Other people were going to the temple, too. It was almost time for prayer.

Peter and John walked up the steps to the temple. They went through the big gate in the outer wall and crossed the first courtyard toward the Beautiful Gate.

As Peter and John got close to the Beautiful Gate, they saw some men carrying a lame man because he could not walk. Every day these men carried the lame man to the Beautiful Gate, where he sat, begging.

The lame man held out his hand and called to people as they passed by. "Money," he called. "Give money to help a poor crippled beggar."

Some people stopped and put money in his outstretched hand. Other people walked on past, pretending they didn't see or hear him. Peter and John slowed down as they got close to the beggar.

The beggar looked at them and held out his hand. "Money," he called. "Give money to help a poor crippled beggar."

"I don't have any money to give you," said Peter. "But I'll give you what I have. In Jesus' name, stand up and walk." Peter reached down and took the man's hand.

Slowly the man stood up. His eyes grew wide as he straightened his legs. His legs felt strong. His ankles felt strong.

Peter let go of the man, and the man stood on his own. Then he walked. Then he skipped. Then he jumped. Then he shouted for joy!

Even Peter and John were laughing as they turned to go into the temple. The man followed them. He was praising God.

People stared at the man as he passed them.

"Is that the beggar?" asked one.

"No, it can't be," said another.

"Look! I think it really *is* the beggar!" said another.

Soon a small crowd gathered around Peter and John and the man who had been healed. The people realized that this was the same man they had seen every day, begging at the gate. They were amazed to see him walk.

Seeing so many people gathered around, Peter told them about Jesus. And many of the people believed in Jesus that day. Especially the man who had once been a lame beggar.

On the Desert Road

ACTS 8:26-39

The wheels of the carriage rolled steadily across the road. The driver of the carriage tried to hold the horses to an even pace. *Trot, trot, trot, trot.* He wanted to keep the ride as smooth as he could, because the man riding in the back of the carriage was reading.

The man riding in the carriage was an important man. He was the chief money keeper for Queen Candace of Ethiopia. This man believed in God. He had been to the big city of Jerusalem to worship God. Now he was going back home, down the long desert road to the south. As he rode, he read Scriptures that told about God.

At first there had been many travelers on this road. But as they got farther away from the city, there were fewer and fewer people to meet. So the money keeper read. And the horses trot, trot, trotted. And the wheels of the carriage rolled on.

Now an angel had come to one of Jesus' followers named Philip. The angel had told Philip, "Go south on the desert road." So Philip was traveling south on the desert road at the same time that the carriage was traveling south.

When Philip saw the carriage, the Holy Spirit told Philip, "Go over and walk beside the carriage." So Philip ran over to the carriage and began to walk beside it.

Philip heard the money keeper reading out loud. "Hello," said Philip. "Do you understand what you are reading?"

The money keeper shook his head. "How can I understand it?" he asked. "I don't have anyone to explain it to me. But come up into my carriage and sit with me, and we can talk about it."

So Philip climbed up into the carriage and sat beside the man.

The money keeper read, "He was led out to be killed. He did not fight back. He did not argue." Then the man looked at Philip. "Who is this talking about?" he asked.

Philip knew that these Scriptures were about Jesus. So Philip told the money keeper all about Jesus as the carriage rumbled down the desert road.

Suddenly the money keeper said, "Look!"

Philip looked.

The man was pointing to a pond. "There's some water," he said. "I can be baptized!"

The man ordered his driver to stop the carriage. Then the money keeper and Philip climbed out and walked to the pond. They waded into the water. Philip dipped the money keeper in the water very quickly, baptizing him.

After they came up out of the water, the money keeper climbed back into his carriage. The driver called to the horses and snapped the reins. And once again the carriage rumbled south down the desert road. But now the money keeper riding home in the carriage was full of joy!

Peter and the Angel

ACTS 12:5-17

It was dark. There was no bed. There was no pillow. Peter had to sleep in a jail, chained between two soldiers. There were other guards at the door.

Peter had been telling people about Jesus. And the mean king didn't like that. That's why Peter was in the jail.

But Peter's friends were together praying. They were asking God to save Peter.

Back at the dark jail, Peter was asleep. All of a sudden, a bright light shone in the jail. And an angel was standing there!

The angel tapped Peter on his side. Peter opened his eyes and looked at the angel. "Hurry!" said the angel. "Get up!"

The chains on Peter's wrists fell off. "Put your clothes on," said the angel. "And your sandals."

So Peter put his clothes on—and his sandals.

"Now put your coat on and follow me," said the angel.

So Peter followed the angel. But Peter thought he was dreaming. He didn't know it was really happening.

The angel led Peter past the first guards. The angel led Peter past the next guards. Then they came to an iron gate. This was the gate that led to the city. All by itself, the gate opened. The angel led Peter through the gate and down the dark street. And suddenly the angel left.

Then Peter said, "Now I understand! The Lord sent his angel to save me!"

Peter hurried to Mary's house. His friends were there praying for him. Peter knocked at the door.

A girl named Rhoda came to the door. "Who is it?" she asked.

"It's me. Peter," he answered.

Rhoda was so surprised and excited that she forgot to open the door. Instead, she ran to tell Peter's friends. "It's Peter! He's at the door!" she said.

"You're crazy," they said. "Peter is in jail."

"No, really," said Rhoda. "It really is Peter."

They said, "It must be his angel."

But Peter knocked and knocked and knocked some more.

Finally they went back to the door and opened it. When they saw Peter, they were amazed!

Peter quietly told them how the angel had led him out of the jail. And for the rest of the night, Peter got to sleep in a real, soft, warm bed.

The Night the Ground Shook

ACTS 16:11-40

The river rippled along, swirling and flowing and lapping at the rocks and grasses along its banks. Trees dipped their branches as the breeze ruffled their leaves.

Paul and some of his friends made their way down the path to the river. Silas was one of the people with Paul. They had heard that there was a place by the river where people gathered to pray. It was much quieter there than in the big busy city of Philippi.

As Paul and his friends walked along the riverbank, they found

a group of women. One of these women was Lydia, who sold purple cloth in the city. Lydia loved God, but she had not heard about Jesus, God's Son. So Paul told her and the other women about Jesus.

Lydia believed Paul, and he baptized her in the river. Then Lydia invited Paul and his friends to her house. So they stayed with Lydia and her family for many days.

One day as Paul and Silas and the others were on their way to the place of prayer, they heard someone shouting behind them. They turned around to see a girl—a fortune-teller who was controlled by an evil spirit. She was shouting, "These men serve God Most High. They are here to tell you how to be saved!"

Every day this girl followed Paul and his friends, shouting the same thing. At last Paul was tired of this. He turned around and told the evil spirit to leave her. And it did. The girl became calm again.

But this girl had worked for some men who made money from

her fortune-telling. Now that she couldn't tell fortunes anymore, these men were angry. They grabbed Paul and his friend Silas, marching them down the street to the crowded, noisy marketplace. The men yelled to the city leaders that Paul and Silas had been teaching people to do wrong things.

More and more people gathered around. Finally some guards came and took Paul and Silas to jail. The guards warned the jailer not to let Paul and Silas get away. So the jailer put them into a jail cell deep inside the prison.

By now it was getting dark. Paul and Silas knew they didn't need to go to a place of prayer to worship God. So they began singing and praying right there in jail.

Around midnight the ground began to rumble and shake. The locked chains of all the prisoners fell off, and the jail doors flew open.

When the jailer saw what was happening, he thought all the prisoners would run away. He was afraid he would be in big trouble!

But Paul called, "We are all still here."

The jailer called for his helpers to bring lamps. Sure enough, no one had run away. The jailer got down on his knees in front of Paul and Silas. "What should I do now?" he asked.

"Believe in Jesus," said Paul. "Then you will be saved."

So the jailer took Paul and Silas into his house. He and his family let Paul baptize them. All of the people in the jailer's family were very glad that they knew about Jesus now.

Paul and Silas were glad, too. They spent the rest of the night at the jailer's house. And the next day Paul and Silas went back to Lydia's house.

Looking into Heaven

REVELATION 1; 4; 21–22

Sea waves splashed onto the shore. Sea breezes blew across the beach. It was an island. Jesus' friend John lived there. He watched the waves splash. He felt the breezes blow. And he thought about Jesus, his best friend.

One day, while he was thinking about Jesus, John heard a loud voice behind him. It said, "Write what you see, and make it into a book."

When John turned around to see who was talking, he saw a man in a long robe and a wide gold belt. It was Jesus! He was holding seven stars. And he was shining like a bright light!

Jesus said, "You will see what is going to happen. Write it down."

Then John saw many, many amazing things. He saw God sitting on a big white throne. A rainbow circled around the throne. John heard thousands and thousands of angels praising Jesus.

And John heard a voice from the throne. "God is going to live with people now. He will wipe away all the tears from their eyes. No one will ever die here, or get hurt here, or cry here. All the bad things will be gone. Everything will be new!"

Then John saw God's big new city. It had a big high wall. In the wall were 12 gates made out of pearls. And an angel stood at each gate. Nothing bad could come inside. But God's people could come in.

Inside the city the street was made of gold so shiny that it looked like glass. The city didn't need a sun or moon because God was the light.

Right through the middle of the street of that city there was a river, crystal clean. A special tree grew on each side of it. It was the tree of life, and it had 12 different kinds of fruit.

In that city God's people can always see him. And he will take care of them forever. There won't be any more night. God will be their light. And they will live like kings there forever and ever.

When John had seen these things, an angel said to him, "You can believe what you saw. It's true."

Then Jesus said, "I sent my angel to show you all of this. I am called the bright morning star."

John wrote all these things. Then he wrote, "Come. Anyone who wants to come can come to Jesus, and Jesus will be that person's best friend forever and ever."

Song List

1. Do You Remember?
2. Baby Moses
3. Feather Bed
4. Glorious, Glorious
5. Be Still
6. The Lord Is My Shepherd
7. Dream of Heaven
8. All God's Children Praise
9. Father, Father
10. I Love You, Lord
11. No Roars Tonight
12. We're Glad to Be Your Children
13. Now the Sun Slips Away
14. God Knows Me
15. In the Darkness of the Night
16. Sleepy, Sleepy Tiger
17. Come, Little Children, Come
18. Look at All God Made
19. God Will Watch over Me
20. Tiny Baby
21. I'll Sing You a Dream
22. You Planned for Children
23. We Are Full of Joy

Look for all these great resources from Karyn Henley!

VIDEOS

Down by the Station
0-8423-3446-7

Grow, Grow, Grow
0-8423-5241-4

I Feel Like a Giggle
0-8423-3445-9

I Feel Like a Giggle DVD
Bonus Pack
0-8423-8696-3

Five Little Ladybugs
0-8423-3444-0

Five Little Ladybugs DVD
Bonus Pack
0-8423-8694-7

Noah's Zoo
0-8423-5255-4

Noah's Zoo DVD
Bonus Pack
0-8423-8695-5

BOOKS

Gram's Song
0-8423-7669-0

My Learn-to-Pray Bible
0-8423-8733-1

My Thank-You Bible
0-8423-5376-3

Rag Baby
0-8423-5434-4

BIBLES
AND DEVOTIONALS

Day by Day Kid's Bible
0-8423-5536-7

Day by Day Devotions
0-8423-7485-X

Day by Day Devotions 2
0-8423-7486-8
COMING FALL 2005!

www.karynhenley.com